The
Woman
You're
Made
to Be

SHE

SAFE HEALTHY EMPOWERED

Rebecca St. James and
Lynda Hunter Bjorklund

 Tyndale House Publishers, Inc. ✴ Wheaton, IL

Library of Congress Cataloging-in-Publication Data

St. James, Rebecca.
  She : the woman you're made to be / Rebecca St. James and Lynda Hunter Bjorklund.
    p. cm.
  Includes bibliographical references.
  ISBN 1-4143-0026-3 (sc)
1. Christain women—Religious life. 2. Femininity—Religious aspects—Christianity. I. Bjorklund, Lynda Hunter. II. Title.
  BV4527.S725 2004
  248.8'43—dc22   2004011776

Printed in the United States of America

08 07 06 05 04
 5   4   3   2   1

TABLE OF CONTENTS

"I feel so vulnerable."

"I don't like my body!"

"I can't keep up at home or at work."

"I've got to prove myself."

"Why do I feel so alone?"

"I feel anxious when I think about the future."

"I don't want to be hurt again."

"I can't let go of guilt from my past."

"Who's really there for me?"

"I feel so out of control!"

"Am I making a difference?"

FROM THE AUTHORS

You may have picked up this book because you've recently made statements or asked questions similar to these, either silently or aloud. Most of us have. Life for us as modern women can be confusing and overwhelming. Culture says one thing, our heart tells us another, and pressures threaten to overtake us:

> pressures to compromise
> > pressures to be strong and independent
> > > pressures to be superwomen

Sometimes we feel like time bombs. When we explode, the shrapnel flies at everyone in our path, crippling us and damaging our relationships.

No one is immune to life's upheavals. And no matter how many achievements we're commended for or how together we appear to others, there's still a place in our heart that's exposed to insecurity, anxiety, and the constant demand to perform better. When those distractions interrupt our lives, we need real change.

We believe God is the source of that type of change. The Bible promises it[1], and we've seen Him prove it in the lives of countless women. We've experienced His comfort and wisdom ourselves. And in the process, we've realized that God doesn't want us to merely survive. He truly does have a fulfilled and joyous life waiting for us in the midst of all the challenges.[2]

So come join us! Let's sit down together. Let's expose the lies that Satan uses to bind and confuse us. Let's uncover the truths that can set us free. Let's go after God's best.

And let's become the SHEs God designed us to be.

—Rebecca and Lynda

"Daily I live with [one] fear—a healthy fear. . . . [It is] that I will miss something God has for me. . . . I don't want to be robbed of even one of God's riches by not taking time to let Him invade my life. By not listening to what He is telling me. By allowing the routine, pressing matters of my minutes to bankrupt me of time for the most exciting, most fulfilling relationship in life."

Carole Mayhall *From the Heart of a Woman* [1]

> "This is now bone of my bones and flesh of my flesh; SHE shall be called 'woman.'"
>
> **Genesis 2:23, NIV (emphasis added)**

Chapter 1

Who Is SHE?

Something's wrong. The modern woman is on major overload. She struggles to find time in her day to swap hats among the numerous ones she wears:

* Wife
* Caregiver
* Employee
* Mother
* Taxi Driver
* Housekeeper
* Volunteer
* Teacher
* Neighbor
* Chef
* Counselor
* Friend

And as she fights to catch her breath between all her duties, she is bombarded with conflicting messages every time she turns on the TV, fixes dinner, runs on her treadmill, or sits down to a meeting at work. These messages attempt to define where she fits in the world, as well as her relationships, her spirituality, and her very identity as a woman. She

she\'she\ *pronoun* 1: The use of lowercase *she* indicates the informal title every female receives the moment she is born.

SHE\'SHE\ *pronoun* 1: The use of the uppercase *SHE* is a title bestowed on those women who seek more from God, submit themselves to His transforming work, and commit to a lifetime of being reborn into His original design. The result is a safe, healthy, and empowered SHE.

struggles to feel beautiful when she's probably not the superfit woman the media portrays as ideal. Intimacy eludes her, and the feeling of being unprotected overwhelms her in a generation ravaged by the breakdown of the family. She wrestles with loneliness in an age that has lost the art of mentoring. She is confused in trying to figure out what it means to be truly feminine amidst the feminist messages screaming all around her. Purity of both body and mind is a battle for the married as well as the unmarried, and the younger as well as the older woman—when sex sells and the world treats it so casually. She finds physical, emotional, and spiritual boundaries rare or nonexistent. Purpose is difficult to discover in a time that glorifies worldly success and downplays faithfulness to family, friends, and God. And freedom is tough to find even for the woman who has fought to overcome past hurts and baggage.

It's no wonder she struggles!

Maybe you've read books, listened to talk shows, or joined Bible studies to find answers to the dilemma of the modern woman. Whatever the case, you know what it's like to be her, right? Like every other woman alive today, you have a lot on your plate. You want to be your best, give and get the most from life . . . but just what does that mean? And *how* do you accomplish those things?

Women are crying out for answers that today's culture simply isn't giving. Fortunately, we can know where to find the truth about what it means to be a modern woman. And in that truth, we're sure to discover the help we're all looking for in this adventure called life.

Before we dive in to the heart of this subject, let's back up for a minute. We as its authors see this book as a journey, a coming together of sisters from different walks and backgrounds. It's a joining of hands and hearts to access God's practical, empowering truths for our life today. Between the two of us, our individual life experiences have brought us to a place where we've seen the need for a book like this one.

REBECCA ✳ I'm originally from Australia, but for the last ten years I've traveled as a Christian music writer and performer, so I've had lots of opportunities to meet women from all over the world. I, like so many of the women I've met, love being a woman. The mix of femininity, a caring and nurturing spirit, strength, and sensitivity we are naturally gifted with is a joyful thing for me. Though I'm fulfilling many of my life goals now, I love dreaming about my future husband and how it will feel to be protected and treasured by him. I imagine one day being a mother and teaching my own kids the lessons I've learned through my adventurous life and my role as the oldest of seven children. ✳

LYNDA ✳ I love being a woman too, but having lived nearly twice the number of years Rebecca has, I see my SHEness through slightly different eyes. And I've realized that life doesn't always turn out as we hoped it would.

I did find and marry my Prince Charming—Sir David is his name—but not until I had put in more than fourteen years as a single mom. Through my work as an author and an editor of Focus on the Family's *Single-Parent Family* magazine, I heard from women from nearly every continent about their struggles, concerns, and the things that kept them from celebrating life to the fullest. I found myself constantly amazed at the different stories that all echoed a common search for our identity as women, our spirituality, and an overall balance in life. ✳

SHE refers to a woman, uniquely and wonderfully made. Not only are we distinctly different from men, but every woman is an original and unlike any other female in history. Our differences are something to celebrate and something that the two of us have enjoyed while writing this book!

Lynda is married; Rebecca is single. Rebecca looks forward to having children, while Lynda looks forward to the patter of grandchildren's feet. Rebecca deals with PMS, and Lynda deals with hot flashes. Neither of us has heard of the music the other listens to. Rebecca goes to sleep at night a few hours before Lynda gets up each morning.

Yet we're both modern women just like you, trying to find balance and joy and purpose in life. Our differences represent the brilliant mosaic of womanhood. Our lives join at the depth of our common passion to be safe, healthy, and empowered SHEs who live each day to the fullest and help set the pace for future generations of women.

SHEdom

Now that you know a bit about us, let's get back to the question, who is she/SHE?

On a field trip to a large bookstore chain, we discovered that some of the most popular books and magazines for women reflect the stressed-out, hurting, searching feelings of our time. Many magazine titles such as *Glamour, Self, More, Black Book,* and *Millionaire* appeal to our culture's self-centeredness. And books addressing our never-ending desire for self-improvement have become best sellers:

❋ *Self Matters: Creating Your Life from the Inside Out,* Dr. Phil McGraw (New York: Free Press, 2001)

❋ *Excuse Me, Your Life Is Waiting: The Astonishing Power of Feelings,* Lynn Grabhorn (Charlottesville, Va.: Hampton Roads Publishing Co., 2000)

The common theme that struck us most, however, was the many titles we saw that addressed the failure of the feminist movement and the overwhelming load we have convinced ourselves we need to carry. *Talk* magazine featured an article titled "Love, Sex, Family, Career—It was all supposed to be so easy for the modern woman!"

We found editor and compiler Cathi Hanauer particularly intriguing, as she emphasized the common theme of dissatisfaction. She writes: "Women today have more choices than at any time in history, yet many smart, ambitious, contemporary women are finding themselves angry, dissatisfied, stressed-out."[2]

She quotes Kristin van Ogtrop in the same book:

> *Here are a few things people have said about me at the office:*
> *"You're unflappable." "Are you ever in a bad mood?" Here are*
> *things people—okay, the members of my family—have said about*
> *me at home: "Mommy is always grumpy." "Why are you so tense?"*
> *"You're too mean to live in this house and I want you to go back to*
> *work for the rest of your life!"*[3]

Danielle Crittenden, founder and editor of *The Women's Quarterly* magazine, authored a best-selling book called *What Our Mothers Didn't Tell Us: Why Happiness Eludes the Modern Woman*. Crittenden writes: "Talk to women under forty today, and you will hear that in spite of the fact that they have achieved goals previous generations of women could only dream of, they nonetheless feel more confused and more insecure than ever."[4] This author goes on to examine big topics in the life of a woman: sex, marriage, motherhood, work, aging, and politics. She argues that a generation of women has been misled—taught to blame men and pursue independence at all costs. "Happiness is obtainable," Crittenden says, "but only if women will free their minds from outdated feminist attitudes."[5]

Unfortunately, Christian women haven't fared much better. In fact, Christian women can struggle even more with depression and anxiety than women who don't know God. Not only do we experience the heavy demands of family, work, and self that all women face, but on top of this, many of us feel that we can't show our weakness or confusion. A Christian woman surely should not feel overwhelmed, angry, and at times (gasp!) bitter. As a result, we heap guilt and shame on ourselves. And our discouragement grows.

REBECCA ✳ Recently I attended the graduation of a friend who had finished an in-depth biblical healing course through a well-known ministry. As I watched the graduation unfold, I couldn't help but pick up on the untouchable aura surrounding the ministry's female president. Here was a woman who epitomized the successful modern female. She had a flourishing, worldwide ministry; she was trim and toned; she was a confident leader. But instead of being impressed by her accomplishments and leadership, I left the ceremony feeling sorry for her. She exuded a hard, overly independent, "I can do it all" air about her that seemed to push me away. I felt that deep inside her tough shell was a sensitive, insecure woman who had been lost in the midst of being strong for everyone else. ✳

We all battle this tendency toward cultural hardness in a world where Satan's lies about womanhood run rampant. When we look around us, we see the turmoil in the eyes of women everywhere. Somewhere deep inside of us is the knowledge that this is not what God wants for us. Something *is* wrong! Will the real SHE please stand up?

Womanhood Redefined

We haven't found all the answers, and we're not here to wallow in our pain, share our communal tears, or simply feel better. This book isn't a quick fix, but rather an encouragement for us to rethink the ways we define and live out our womanhood. We're looking for something permanent—a new way of viewing ourselves and our role in the world, in our family, and in our career. We're looking for a new perspective on what it means to be both strong and feminine, gentle and assertive, compassionate and inspiring, nurturing and nurtured. It's a perspective that flies in the face of the feminist jargon that has subtly impacted us in ways we may not even realize.

For now, let's toss aside the self-help books and magazines and go straight to the timeless truths found in the Bible. After all, who better to know what a woman should be than God, who created us?

The Bible teaches that we can experience real and lasting change only by looking to God and allowing Him to change us. Yes, we might in our own power be able to set better boundaries, build more discipline into our lives, and raise our self-esteem as the magazine headlines at the grocery checkout lines promise. But the Bible says that God offers the way to permanent change and real joy, hope, and peace.[6]

As we prepared to write this book, we made a trip to Breckenridge, Colorado, for a week of undistracted work. Girl, how we suffered for the ministry there in our ski lodge! During that time, we compiled a list of both *our* felt needs and the concerns we'd heard from other women around the world through e-mails, letters, and personal contact. We also threw into the mix quotes, magazine articles, excerpts from books we'd read, and Scriptures we'd discovered. We input this information into the computer, printed it, and literally cut it up and placed it randomly across the floor of our cabin. Then we organized the copy into categories as it seemed to fit. Out of that exercise and a lot of prayer, we uncovered nine key areas of particular struggle for today's women:

* Protection   * Beauty   * Mentorship

* Intimacy   * Purity   * Boundaries

* Femininity   * Freedom   * Purpose

Then we went out to dinner, praying that God would show us our title for this book. Soon we had not only our title, but the overarching themes the book would cover as well:

Safety
Health
Empowerment

And so *SHE* was born.

The common thread woven throughout is that we as women have believed certain lies—lies the Bible says Satan throws at us.[7] What's the result? Mediocre, overcommitted, self-centered, ineffective, and joyless living.

But, thankfully, there's hope. It's time to redefine feminism. We call it the "new feminism"—a rediscovery of the timeless truths for moving beyond lies that weigh us down, pressure us, and stress us out. No longer will those lies keep us from breaking free of the nagging claws of exhaustion, dissatisfaction, lack of fulfillment, and anger. As a result, we can live what the Bible calls "abundant" life.[8] Together, let's peel back the layers and discover all God wants for us as women.

Jesus Himself reveals that the secret to transforming from an unsafe, unhealthy, and unempowered she to a safe, healthy, and empowered SHE is in refusing to fall for the lies of Satan and, instead, embracing and living out God's truths. In John 8, Jesus warns us about the bad news of the lie:

> [The devil] was a murderer from the beginning and has always hated the truth. There is no truth in him. When he lies, it is consistent with his character; for he is a liar and the father of lies.[9]

But Jesus also gave us the good news:

> You will know the truth, and the truth will set you free.[10]

God is good and loving and greater than all the circumstances, relationships, and heartaches that threaten to overwhelm us. All we have to do is recognize the lies and replace them with truths. That's when freedom comes.

The Beginnings of SHE

Jesus was known for applying timeless truths to contemporary life in ways that people could understand. So let's follow His lead and go back to the beginning to understand the way it was supposed to be before everything went wrong.

First there was God, who made Himself a world. He filled His special place with all the beautiful things in the heavens, in the waters, and on the earth. And He described it all as "good." But God wanted more. He wanted the "very good." He also wanted someone made in His image to whom He could show His love. So He created man and assigned him the job of naming everything that He had created. Then God made woman, a "helper comparable to [man]."[11]

Man and woman were bonded together as one in a lifelong, committed relationship. They were naked in who they were before God and each other. They were not ashamed because they were not distracted by things that didn't please God—not ashamed and distracted, that is, until sin cut into their world and enticed them to look away from God's truths and toward Satan's lies.

Satan promised power and wisdom and beauty and life. But as soon as the couple fell for his act, their bond was divided. Their eyes were opened, and they felt ashamed and tried to hide from God. No longer could they be naked and unashamed before their Maker.

The man blamed the woman. The woman blamed the snake. The man and the woman—and the snake—were forced to accept the consequences of rejecting what was right for the temporary pleasure of what looked good but was actually wrong. The deception led to separation from God and eventually to death.

This is the heritage that Eve, the first she, passed on to all the other shes to follow. God's best—a pure and full life—was given as a gift in the beginning but became a prize to be sought after like mad by all the women who have followed.

But someday God will return and make Himself a new world. He'll fill it with special HEs and SHEs who chose to live their life His way—whole and unashamed before Him. Together we'll exist forever, free from mistakes and wrongs and confusion. Any of us who choose to know Him will one day experience real freedom and (snake-free!) joyful life with Him. Until then, lots of snakes run wild, tempting and trying to pull us away from God's best and even costing us our life.

All of us are on this journey, regardless of the color of our skin, the age of our body, the status of our job, or the nature of our past. Every day we make choices—we can fall for Satan's deceptions and try to hide our mistakes from God, or we can ask for His guidance and begin to follow His ways.

LYNDA ✳ I admire the Rebeccas in my life, who have chosen from their earliest days to stay on the naked-and-unashamed paths before God. I didn't. Though raised in a Christian home, I "ate the fruit" when I was about twenty-one years old, which sent me down paths that led away from God. More than a decade of wrong choices followed, robbing me of the joy and wholeness I had felt from God in my younger days. Then fear of facing the future as a single mom without God's guidance brought me back to Him. In September 1985, I took a walk in the field behind my home with a Bible tucked under my arm, sat down on a rock, and looked up at the sky. I asked God to forgive my sins and to take over my life—not just my single-parent needs. That prayer changed my life and has affected everything for me since. The experience left me with a driving passion to help other women choose God's ways and avoid making similar mistakes. I also want you to get to know the good God I've come to know. When we mess up, He's ready to forgive us, heal us, and help us move on in a relationship with Him. I bring that passion to my part in writing this book. I want to grow with you as we become the SHEs that God planned from the beginning. ✳

So what qualities did the first woman possess that God can help you and me regain? Before Eve's first sin, SHE was **S**afe, **H**ealthy, and **E**mpowered. We can be too.

Safe: To Be Held Securely

In the original Garden, Eve never worried about her safety. When we are safe, we are freed from risk, danger, harm, and injury.

REBECCA ✳ I learned the meaning of safety from a little girl in Ecuador when I joined my brother Joel on a trip to meet the child he sponsors through Compassion International. We visited the smiling Compassion children in remote villages, helping to serve food at one of the projects and singing worship songs as we traveled by bus through beautiful, mountainous scenery. In one village classroom, my attention was drawn to a little girl about eight years old. A large, blanketed lump covered almost half of her small frame. With her permission, I furrowed into the blankets and discovered the tiny face of a baby who was only weeks old. At the intrusion to her safe little haven and the awakening by cold air and a strange face, the baby started to cry. The substitute "mom," whom I later discovered was the infant's cousin, quickly took the child to her real mother, who was a teacher at the project.

It hit me that in similar ways, I too long to be protected, cocooned in love, and tucked away from danger. ✳

Security is a basic human need. But either intentionally or unintentionally, people and circumstances jerk back our covers of safety and expose us to the cold winds of life. That exposure destroys our sense of security and leaves us feeling vulnerable to further danger. To compensate, we scramble to other sources of protection, hoping to regain some sense of safety.

We women can be especially susceptible to this coping mechanism simply because crime rates prove that women are often targets for predators. But we need emotional safety as well as physical safety. We tend to be fairly in touch with our hurts and feelings. To find emotional security, we often settle for less-than-whole sources, if only for the temporary feeling of being cared for. The media tells us we're strong if we can do it all on our own, so we sacrifice the true intimacy that comes from meaningful relationships and even more so from God. Ultrafeminist views tell us we need to break the glass ceiling to prove our worth, so we accept misconceptions about what it means to be feminine, assuming that to be so would make us even more susceptible to danger.

God, however, offers us real safety from the storms that life blows our way. It's possible to know that you are being cradled by God, held warm and tight in His arms through all circumstances.

> **LYNDA** ✻ I once read a story about a chicken coop that caught fire. Once the flames had been extinguished, people who were sorting through the remains found a hen with her wings spread across the nest to protect her eggs. Though the mother perished, the protection she had provided allowed her eggs to make it safely through the danger. ✻

Jesus provided a similar image in Matthew 23:37. He told Jerusalem how much He wanted to gather His people together and shelter them as a mother hen does her chicks. Jesus wants to do the same for us today. We can continue to fight the fires on our own by relying on other people and things, or we can crawl under His wings. The Bible tells us, "He will shield you with his wings. He will shelter you with his feathers. His faithful promises are your armor and protection."[12]

In the coming chapters we'll discuss how this is possible: how to become a protected, feminine, wholly safe woman whose heart knows firsthand the joy of true intimacy.

Healthy: Check the Pulse of Your Life

Feeling safe and cared for is only one part of being complete. Being emotionally healthy is another big must.

> **LYNDA** ✻ When my husband left, I was pregnant with my third child, and my girls were one and three. I didn't want to be divorced, so my natural reaction was to curl up in a ball, feel sorry for myself, and nurse my wounds. But one day, my little boy rolled over for the first time and my two girls chased each other through the house. I realized at that point my children were excited about this business of living, and I needed to be there for them. Holding on to my hurts would only perpetuate more hurts and poor choices that would affect all of us. In order to raise healthy children, I needed to get healthy myself. So the becoming-healthy process began for me. ✻

To be healthy is to be strong and thriving, able to bounce back from tough times. And tough times can be plentiful. Society constantly tells us to look good on the outside whatever the cost. It also tells us to go ahead and do whatever feels good, which breaks down the rules of our conduct. And when it comes to reactions to other people's wrong treatment of us, the world tells us we're justified however we respond. If we heed this kind of advice, we'll never bounce back from the hardship.

To make things worse, the self-centered theme of our day marches on screaming such propaganda as "Have it your way" and "We love to see you smile." These messages result in one of two responses in us: We say, "It's my turn now," and pursue our own desires, regardless of who we have to hurt, neglect, or trample in the process; or we decide, "It will never be my turn," and we continue serving, overcommitting, and neglecting our own dreams and desires—all the while feeling life has gypped us of the things we deserve.

Either way, we sink into unhealthy responses that leave us with unresolved feelings and emotions and keep us from moving on with our life.

However, God offers another choice. The Bible says that He brings health to us—"'I will give you back your health and heal your wounds,' says the Lord"[13]—and that He wants us to prosper and be in good health.[14]

Beautiful, pure, and *free* can be words to describe our emotional, physical, and spiritual health—when we let God heal our wounds and teach us how to conduct our life.

Empowered: Having What It Takes

Finally, a safe and healthy woman is on her way to having what it takes to live an empowered life. She knows her limits, she invites learning from other women who've been where she is, and she knows what she's about and Who she's living for.

> **REBECCA** * On a family vacation years ago, I learned to windsurf. For someone who had never surfed before, this experience could have ended in disaster, but fortunately it didn't.

We were staying on the lovely Sunshine Coast in Queensland, Australia. The weather was beautiful, the beach lay just a few minutes' walk away, and the sparkling lake beckoned me. I was determined to conquer the Windsurfer and not let it conquer me. So after a few lessons from the instructor, I gave it a go. I lost my balance a few times, but eventually I found myself sailing solo across the water, feeling the exhilaration of being powered and propelled by the wind.

This windsurfing thing required some serious concentration for a novice like me. Each muscle had to stay alert and work overtime. But even an experienced windsurfer would say that to really go places, to be fully powered by the wind, you must be focused and listen to instruction, apply strong concentration, and put consistent effort into it. Unless your objective is to slow down or stop, you have to give it all you've got. ✻

Trusting yourself completely to God and then giving the Christian life all you've got is what it takes to be an empowered woman. To experience all the freedom and joy God has in store for you, you can't coast or stop. None of us can. We must keep moving by allowing God to empower us, and He does that by changing us. Through mentoring, He allows other godly people to teach us. Through building godly boundaries, we prevent intrusions from dangerous people and events. Through discovering and pursuing our God-given purpose, we stay on track and away from distractions that take our focus off of Him and that rob us of the power He offers.

As you allow God to change you in these areas, negative people and situations can change as well. Conflicts are settled; obstacles are destroyed. Instead of wasting time and energy waiting for other people and circumstances to change, you can remain empowered as you count on God to change *you*. How freeing to know that your empowerment depends on no one but God. You'll see that reality develop as a major theme of our book.

> Instead of wasting time and energy waiting for other people and circumstances to change, you can remain empowered as you count on God to change *you*. How freeing to know that your empowerment depends on no one but God.

God's kind of empowerment means He's the One who invests, authorizes, and equips us. In a world that emphasizes power, it seems contradictory to us that as we let go of the controls and give them to

God, He actually empowers us. But that's the way He works. He provides the power: "God is awesome in his sanctuary. The God of Israel gives power and strength to his people. Praise be to God!"[15]

You can apply diligence and consistent effort to be the mentored, boundaried, and purposeful daughter God intends you to be. Then you'll see the sails of your life fill with God's wind, propelling you to new, totally empowered destinations with Him.

Twenty Questions

Before we can find safety, health, or empowerment, we need to understand where we've been unsafe, unhealthy, and unempowered in the past. Take a look at the questions below. Be as honest with yourself as possible. Try not to overthink the questions. Your immediate response is usually the most valid. From 0 to 5, choose where you stand, rating as follows:

0=never   1=rarely   3=sometimes   5=always

1. How often do you feel overwhelmed with feelings of anger or hurt?

0   1   2   3   4   5
Never   Always

2. How regularly do you experience immoral thoughts or temptations?

0   1   2   3   4   5
Never   Always

3. Do you struggle with fear when it comes to allowing others to know the real you?

0   1   2   3   4   5
Never   Always

4. How often do you say yes to unnecessary demands?

0   1   2   3   4   5
Never   Always

5. How often do you feel that your life is out of balance?

0   1   2   3   4   5
Never   Always

6. Do you feel unsure about your unique giftings and purpose on earth?

0	1	2	3	4	5
Never					Always

7. Do you hold on to disappointments and find it hard to forgive?

0	1	2	3	4	5
Never					Always

8. Do you feel offended or uncomfortable with a man's chivalrous acts, such as when he offers to open a door for you?

0	1	2	3	4	5
Never					Always

9. How often do you feel dissatisfied in the area of your own spiritual growth?

0	1	2	3	4	5
Never					Always

10. How often do you struggle with your self-image?

0	1	2	3	4	5
Never					Always

11. How often do you watch, listen to, or read things that contain impurity?

0	1	2	3	4	5
Never					Always

12. How often do you feel envious of another woman's appearance, either in real life or in the media?

0	1	2	3	4	5
Never					Always

13. Is there a lack of mentoring (both giving and receiving) in your life?

0	1	2	3	4	5
Never					Always

14. How often do you struggle with needing people too much or too little?

0	1	2	3	4	5
Never					Always

15. Do you feel vulnerable at home or at work?

0	1	2	3	4	5
Never					Always

16. How often do you feel discouraged or attacked by the enemy?

0	1	2	3	4	5
Never					Always

17. How often do you feel snowed under by your own and others' expectations of you?

0	1	2	3	4	5
Never					Always

18. How often do you feel unworthy of God's love?

0	1	2	3	4	5
Never					Always

19. Does your family make you feel unsafe emotionally?

0	1	2	3	4	5
Never					Always

20. Do you ever think there must be more to who you are and more to life than what you're living?

0	1	2	3	4	5
Never					Always

Now add up your score.

1–25 You are amazing! With God's power, you have been standing strong amidst incredible cultural pressure. You have a godly perspective on life and are strong in His power. Keep on keeping on.

26–50 You're doing well. This book will be a good reminder for you in areas you understand, but you can always grow and deepen.

51–75 We're glad you're reading this book! You're obviously seeking help in many areas, and God will speak His wisdom and truth into your unique life situation.

76–100 Sister . . . it's time to figure out some important things! The coming chapters will give you a lot of biblical insight and help, but they should not replace one-on-one mentoring. Don't wait! As soon as possible, seek out a wise, older godly woman and share your heart with her. And please don't put off getting professional help if necessary. You are too valuable to continue missing out on God's best for you.

This exercise will help you know a little about where you stand today in your quest to live more fully tomorrow. Together, let's start where we are and head to where we can be. Let's become the SHEs God designed us women to be.

✳

Dear God,
I know too well what it's like to be the unsafe, unhealthy, unempowered "she" that I don't want to be anymore. Lord, You've made me aware that there is more to womanhood than what I've seen and experienced. Free me from the burden of my past failures. I long to know completely how much You love me. I want to soak up Your love, finding my security and wholeness in You. Change me, Lord; tear away the old habits. Let the faulty mind-sets melt and be replaced with truth. Break the power Satan's lies have had over me. Help me grow from she to SHE as I trust You to transform my life. I love You, Lord. Do what You want in my heart and mind. In Jesus' name, amen.

✳ **SHEism** ✳ The old "she" ways of thinking and living haven't worked. Only God can make us truly safe, healthy, and empowered. Only God can make us SHE.

Part One
SAFE

"Take a moment to come before your Place of Refuge in prayer and picture yourself in His protective shadow. Imagine yourself finding a safe place in the cleft of the Rock. . . . Then enjoy that unburdened feeling in His shade."

Joni Eareckson Tada *A Quiet Place in a Crazy World*[1]

> "What joy for all who find protection in him!"
>
> **Psalm 2:12**

Chapter 2

Protected: Safe and Sound

REBECCA ✳ A lot of people might think that I live the ideal life. I travel around the world and sing in front of thousands of people who applaud what I do. It looks so easy, so exciting, so wonderful . . . from the outside looking in.

From the inside, however, it's a different story. Only a few close friends and family have seen the turmoil and pain I've felt in this "privileged" life. Since I entered full-time music ministry at the age of sixteen, writing, recording, touring, and performing has been my life. I'm on the road eight or nine months of the year, performing up to two hundred shows, conducting interviews, and adjusting constantly to new faces and places.

In the fall of 1999, after finishing a grueling thirteen-month tour, I decided to fulfill a lifelong dream and go on a short-term mission trip to Romania. For two months, I handed out sandwiches to street kids, played with the children in the girls' home, cleaned, prayed, and did all I could to pour love into these kids. Though the trip was great, it wasn't until afterward that I felt the toll both the yearlong tour and the mission trip had taken on me.

I returned to Nashville feeling disoriented, emotionally vulnerable, and completely spent. Something was wrong inside me, but I didn't know how to fix it. I felt the added pressure of writing songs for a new album, readjusting to normal life, dealing with emotional and physical exhaustion, and because people were watching me, handling the stress and acting as though everything was okay.

My first instinct was to run away and somehow try to escape the inner turmoil. So partly to clear my head and partly because of society's pressure to be independent, I moved out of my family's home into a tiny house in a quaint downtown section of Franklin, Tennessee. I had romantic dreams of getting my life in order, befriending my neighbors, and finally finding some balance. *It'll just be God and me,* I thought. No distractions. Sheltered from the outside storms of life. A little haven. . . . But it was not to be.

I experienced the most horrible time of my life in the quietness of that house. I'd come "home" after a stressful day in the studio to find no one to talk to, no one to care. I grew desperately lonely. I felt disillusioned and unprotected. I believed the lie that I had to handle it all on my own, and in the process, every comfort zone I'd known was stripped away. Even God seemed distant. I cried regularly and prayed in desperation. I remember lying on the floor calling out to Him to show me how to escape that place of darkness and sadness. But I couldn't hear Him say anything in return. The future looked bleak and empty. *What if it's going to be like this for the rest of my life?* I'd think, and then panic would set in even more.

I felt my heart go into self-protection mode. To cope with the pain, I began to shut off and shut down. Feeling like I was going crazy, I shared my situation and pain with my pastor. One of the wise things he said that day was, "Rebecca, is God trustworthy? Then trust Him."

It's amazing how we can overlook such simple truths until we really need them. The power of "God is trustworthy, so trust Him" was like flipping on a switch and shining a beacon of light on me. I finally understood how much I'd been relying on myself, trying to be strong and independent, instead of leaning on God for strength and finding my identity and protection in Him. I saw that I had pulled away from family and the support of godly friends and had lost out because of it.

I did move back home to the community I needed, but more important than the decision I made was the wisdom I found. Through my experience, I learned much about the power and importance of community—that we're made to rely on each other and not to be lone rangers. I realized just how much I had bought into the culture's agenda of over-independence. I also realized that many other women—maybe even you—have gone through much worse traumas than mine and may still be struggling with similar agonies of feeling lonely and unprotected. ✳

Unprotection Revealed

LYNDA ✳ I know some of those "many other women" Rebecca wrote about. And I can relate. We've all felt varying degrees of being unprotected. Rhonda's mother failed to see and protect her daughter from sexual abuse at the hands of her father when Rhonda was a young girl. Connie's husband abandoned her—both physically and financially—for another woman after their eleventh child was born. Susan's church let her down after she had put her heart and passions into her church's women's ministry, only to be misunderstood and asked by her pastor to resign. After confiding in her best friend, Ann learned that her friend had betrayed her confidences. Ellen fell prey to the safe-sex lie culture teaches, and now she deals with the consequences of an STD. Tammy responded, "She can't fall apart! She's my rock!" after her mother had a stroke and died soon after. ✳

Do any of these women sound like you? Maybe one or more of the following questions will hit close to home.

✳ Have you ever depended on someone—or something—who let you down or failed to keep you safe?

✳ Do you feel like important people in your life should have done their job better or been there for you but now they're gone?

✳ Has someone's lie hurt you?

✳ Do you find it hard to trust because of the number of people who have left you or disappointed you?

✳ Have feelings of insecurity kept you from enjoying life and being yourself?

✳ Do you feel alone and unprotected?

     Whether the hurts you've been dealt were as intentional as Connie's husband leaving her or as unintentional as Tammy's mother dying or Rhonda's mother failing to notice what was happening right under her nose, unprotection leaves its ugly imprint on the person remaining in its wake. All of us face the cold realties of unprotection at some time in our life when something or someone tears down our security shield. Sometimes that tear catches us by surprise when we're least prepared to deal with it; other times the shield gets chipped away in stages, one small blow after another until the deepest parts of us are laid open, raw and exposed. However our protection was torn away, here's how the process looks:

Dependency
We trust someone/something and often even depend on them for our safekeeping.

Exposure
The person/thing we thought was safe lets us down and sometimes even causes the attack.

Attack
Hurt occurs at the exposed place.

Damage
Unprotected and attacked, we are left to deal with the consequences.

Response
We shut down, fight back, or develop a pattern of repeating the cycle—unless we find a better way.

It can take years to regain some type of normalcy after a huge loss such as divorce or a loved one's death. The way we process our loss determines how long the healing process takes, how jaded we become, or how willing we are to open ourselves up to future hurts. Injuries can be healed and learned from, or they can become open wounds that never heal and send poison to other areas of our life. If that happens, it's impossible to feel whole and happy as a person or to be able to reach our potential as a woman.

Protection: A Built-In Need

The word *protected* means to be defended, guarded, and sheltered. The two forms of protection we want to focus on in this chapter are physical and emotional. Physical protection guards the body, and emotional protection defends the mind and heart.

> REBECCA ❋ In my case, I was physically safe while living away from my family, but my emotions were ripped apart. Questions plagued me constantly. How did I get to this point? What caused me to hurt so much? Who would keep my heart safe from being hurt so badly again? ❋

All of us, and especially women, have a built-in desire to be protected. Author John Eldredge writes that in the heart of every woman is a desperate desire for three things: to be fought for, wanted, and pursued; to have an adventure to share; and to have beauty to unveil. Men need to be the hero; we need to be the heroine. But woundedness happens to both man and woman. Woundedness disrupts the process and leaves tasks unfulfilled. [2]

In 1954, psychologist Abraham Maslow presented his now well-known hierarchy of needs, which among other things addresses our human desire to feel safe. He separated those needs into three categories: fundamental needs, psychological needs, and self-actualization needs. Maslow believed that before people can fulfill their potential or discover the love, belonging, and self-esteem they want, their fundamental needs have to be satisfied. These fundamental needs, according to Maslow, include food and water—and the need to feel protected.

Maslow's diagram could be compared to our own categories in this book. As we see it, fundamental needs, psychological needs, and self-actualization needs could simply be renamed "safe," "healthy," and "empowered." The diagram could look something like this:

Maslow's—and SHE's—Hierarchy of Needs

SELF-ACTUALIZATION NEEDS
E M P O W E R E D
The need to fulfill one's unique potential

PSYCHOLOGICAL NEEDS
H E A L T H Y
Esteem needs: to achieve, be competent,
and gain approval and recognition
Belongingness and love needs:
to affiliate with others; to be
accepted and belong

FUNDAMENTAL NEEDS
S A F E
Safety needs: to feel secure,
safe, and out of danger
Physiological needs:
to satisfy hunger,
thirst, and sex
drives

We can't move to some of the deeper levels in our quest for SHEness—such as purpose, which we'll cover in chapter 10—until we've addressed the basic, fundamental needs regarding our safety. More than ever before, certain factors work against finding that safety. Transience, the breakdown of marriage, absent fathers, and role confusion all contribute to the loss of our safety. Maybe you've experienced hurts such as these from

❋ your parent, through physical, mental, or emotional abuse or absence;

❋ a friend, through false advice or no advice at all;

❋ your husband, through abandonment or deceit;

❋ your church or pastor, through failure to effectively lead and guard;

❋ culture, through misleading you about your identity as a woman;

❋ God, through appearing to let you down.

Individual experiences like these, combined with global ones such as the terrorist attacks of September 11, 2001, seem to leave us with little reason to feel protected.

As a result, many women have given up on finding safety through others and spend their efforts searching for protection from within. It's easy for an unprotected woman to become hard, independent, selfish, and isolated. Our all-out quest for safety can lead us to counterfeit fixes and crippling attempts to find love, belonging, self-esteem, and the involvement of God in our life. Feminism, materialism, immorality, and obsession with beauty become some of the masks we hide behind as we desperately search for this lost security.

We often don't have much, if any, control over the lack of protection we face, but we do have a say over how we respond. We can allow struggles to destroy us, to put our life on hold, or to propel us into the arms of God.

The first two responses put us on a track of repeating our failures, resisting loving and trusting relationships, and living ineffective lives. To choose to run to the arms of God, however, allows Him not only to soothe the hurts, but to use them for our good and to show us His power. He's been protecting His people since the beginning. Here's one woman's story of God's personal protection.

Hagar: Protection Restored (Genesis 16)

Hagar had worked faithfully for Abram and Sarai for twenty-five years. They, no doubt, became her friends as well as her employers. Hagar probably heard Abram and Sarai talk about God's promise to give them a son in their childless old age. She must have witnessed their discouragement as the years passed without seeing the promise fulfilled and the only thing born to Abram and Sarai were new aches and pains in their ninety- and eighty-year-old bodies.

Then came Sarai's decision to help God out. She told Hagar to sleep with Abram and to give him a son. As always, Hagar obeyed. After all, they were her protectors. She depended on them. She could trust them to know what was best for her, couldn't she? (Obviously not.)

> To choose to run to the arms of God allows Him not only to soothe the hurts, but to use them for our good and to show us His power. He's been protecting His people since the beginning.

Hagar became pregnant, and Sarai became jealous. Through one unprotected act, Hagar's security and shelter were gone, replaced with suffering and rejection from someone she'd likely trusted for years. Not even the law took care of her—it prevented Abram from stepping in and shielding Hagar from Sarai's wrath without Sarai's permission. And Sarai certainly wasn't going to give that!

So Hagar fled to the desert for safety.

Protection and You

Since the early days of humankind, unprotection has turned lives upside down. But so has God's willingness and ability to provide safety. After all protective measures had been stolen from Hagar, she called out to Him and He answered:

> The angel of the Lord found Hagar beside a desert spring. . . . The angel said to her, "Hagar, Sarai's servant, where have you come from, and where are you going?"[3]

God met Hagar in her unprotected place. He knew Hagar's *past* and what she'd been through. He found and cared for her in her *present* situation. And He looked forward with her to her *future*. By the end of this encounter with God in the wilderness, Hagar became convinced of God's love for her:

> I have seen the One who sees me![4]

Let's pause Hagar's story here and skip forward to today. Take a walk in your neighborhood and notice the "Protected by" signs displayed in the front yards, advertising various security companies. While writing this book, we spoke with a friend named Bob, who told us about his home security business.

Since women have always searched for protection, it shouldn't be surprising that when it comes to security systems, we tend to want the whole shebang, while men often prefer to avoid both the cost and the relinquishment of their own role as the protector. Bob said the two main reasons people get a security system are for safety and asset protection; women want the system for protection and men for keeping their property safe.

Just as Bob carefully studies each potential client's home to examine the needs and then to customize a system to fit those needs, you can go to God's Word and find instructions for installing a security system to fit the specifics in your life. By doing that, you can lead a normal, secure life without being preoccupied with an unhealthy search for self-protection.

Now slide your feet into Hagar's sandals. Though God knew her past, present, and future unprotected experiences, she could have denied His provision. Instead, Hagar rejected the lie that He didn't know her or care for her, and she embraced the truth that God was "the One who sees me."

Just as He did for Hagar, God can make good come from the bad things that have happened to you.[5] You and I also need to reject Satan's lies and hold on to God's truths for our own protection:

.... ❋ *SHE Lives the Truth* ❋ ....

1. I need to stay aware that danger lurks around me.

Lie: I haven't experienced a lot of hurt in my life so far, so I don't need a protection plan.

Most people don't bother to build a protection plan into their world. Bob told us that less than 20 percent of homes have a security system. And those numbers are even lower in locations where crime is minimal! But the absence of a security system can leave us with a false sense of security and extremely vulnerable to danger.

You and I can also take our physical, emotional, and relational safety for granted. When we recognize that our enemy Satan prowls "like a roaring lion looking for someone to devour,"[6] we realize that he'll use anything or anybody to accomplish his wickedness, so we have to stay on our toes.

> **REBECCA** ❊ When I went through those awful months that I wrote about earlier in the chapter, I never dreamed I could experience what I did while surrounded by people I loved and trusted. That taught me to be deliberate about building into my life safety nets with God and the people He provides for me, so at any moment I'll be ready to face the lion. ❊

Don't live in fear, but don't live in ignorance, either. Stay on your toes. Keep your eyes open for danger. Be wise about the people you allow into your world. You can never eliminate danger, but you can become wise to it and know how to deal with it when it comes.

2. God is trustworthy, and He provides protection for me.

Lie: Real safety is unattainable because life has taught me that no one is trustworthy.

God offers protection in an abundance of ways. Not only does He provide safety through prayer, the Word, and His peace, He also uses other arms of family and community members to protect us.

God created the family to be a place where we find love, comfort, and security. Each one of us can live toward the goal that God planned for us by being, with His power, the best daughter, sister, wife, and mother we can be. "All of you should be of one mind, full of sympathy toward each other, loving one another with tender hearts and humble minds."[7] These words remind us of the many ways we can help to make our home a place where we both find and give emotional protection, whether we're single or married.

But what happens when that protection and safety we long for are not found within the family?

> **REBECCA** ❊ One friend of mine told me that ever since she could remember, she had functioned in the role of the parent in her

home. Her mom and dad were either absent or too high on drugs or alcohol to care for her. So later in life, she found mentors to take her
under their wing to provide the help and emotional protection she
needed. ✳

In order to avoid settling for counterfeit protection, such as a
compromising male relationship, we need to find godly mentors to
replace the lack of family support. When we ask Him, God shows us
how to look for people who will help provide for our needs of family
and security.

God also provides protection for us through godly community.
"In the multitude of counselors there is safety."[8] If you are willing, this
"multitude of counselors" can help you build an emotional security
system that lets trustworthy people in, but protects you from those
who aren't worthy of your trust. Talk to older, wise Christian women to
help you set the criteria for safe and unsafe people and situations.
Bounce things off of them, such as the way you feel and decisions you
need to make. Once you install your safety system, pay attention to the
alarms and talk to your wise counselors about the uneasiness you feel.

At the end of the day, we have a choice, just as Hagar did: to go
our own way and attempt to protect ourselves alone or to trust completely in God's protection, which includes the extra support of family and community. If you regularly build in these safety measures,
you'll find more security and confidence than you've ever known.

3. God equips me with tools to self-protect in a smart way.

Lie: My protection is dependent on circumstances and everyone around me. I can do nothing.

You've heard the saying "Forewarned is forearmed." Jesus alluded to
this same truth when He forewarned His disciple Peter about Satan's
plans and Peter's need to be prepared, or forearmed: "Satan has asked
to have all of you, to sift you like wheat. But I [Jesus] have pleaded in
prayer for you."[9] Note the way Jesus crafted His words: "Satan has asked
. . ." That means that Satan's attacks have to be filtered through Jesus.

Forewarn yourself means understanding that God has the
ultimate power over the evil that exists around you. Forewarning also

means that Jesus, who has the ultimate power as God's Son, is praying for you and clueing you in to Satan's tricks.

Here are three forearming tools that help in making wise choices. You can arm yourself through your:

CONSCIENCE

God has given you a wonderful protector called the conscience, which Christians know as a tool of the Holy Spirit. But only those who know Jesus as Savior can understand the quiet nudges of His Spirit leading them. We get to know God's voice by spending time daily in prayer and studying the Bible. Here are some situations in which the conscience can provide protection from disaster:

* The married woman turns down a male coworker's seemingly innocent invitation for coffee.

* The single girl decides not to date the non-Christian hunk from college.

* The best friend resists emotional unprotection by confronting a friend's codependency.

INTUITION

> **REBECCA** * From time to time, I've had problems with stalkers. One night before a concert I was told that a suspicious guy who had acted strangely at many of our other shows was there again that evening. Momentarily forgetting this after the concert ended, I began walking backstage alone before my intuition kicked in. I turned back and asked my bass player to walk me to my dressing room. A few minutes later, we discovered the stranger waiting at the bottom of the stairs that led to my room. *

God has given us a mind to use so we can live under wisdom's protective wing. To protect ourselves physically, we can choose not to walk alone at night, even in neighborhoods that seem safe. In an age when codependency and dysfunction are prevalent, we can protect our emotions by listening to our God-given intuition about potentially damaging relationships.

Want other examples of how to use your wise womanly intuition? Not picking up strangers by the side of the road. Not marrying someone who has trouble telling the truth. Not staying at a church where Scripture is being distorted.

SELF-DEFENSE
Today, when date rape and sexual abuse are rampant, learning self-defense may be a good idea for you. The phrase "It's better to be safe than sorry" has never been more applicable.

> **REBECCA** ✳ On a recent trip to Australia, I learned a few self-protection moves from my cousin, who is a black belt in karate. One of my closest friends also has learned self-defense. My local church has offered classes that teach women how to protect ourselves from attack. It's smart to be overprepared in this area. Learning self-defense reminds us not to put ourselves into physically vulnerable situations. ✳

In the same way karate helps with physical protection, you can also learn self-defense methods for emotional safety, such as recognizing danger signs and keeping a guard around your heart. By sharpening and then relying on the gifts God has given you through conscience, intuition, and self-defense, you'll have the tools you need to daily watch out for your own safety.

4. I should be willing to take risks as long as I am guided and protected by God.

Lie: Safety means never taking risks.
Just as a home is never 100 percent protected, you can never completely insulate yourself from danger. As a matter of fact, when you become a Christian, you parachute straight into a war zone. The enemy, Satan, has too much to lose when you are living to please God, so he sets out to destroy you. The difference between this kind of danger and the kind we encounter before we know Christ is that we know our side ultimately wins, and we're fighting the fight for more than the here and now—we're fighting for eternity. While we won't ever be

When you become a Christian, you parachute straight into a war zone. While you won't ever be exempt from the hurts life hurls your way, you can know that because of Christ, you'll never be destroyed.

exempt from the hurts life hurls our way, we can know that because of Christ, we'll never be destroyed. Even if our physical life ends, we have chosen to protect ourselves with that heavenly security system. The code we punch in to engage it properly is a mind-set that says, "This life is not about me, but about You, God. And if I have to endure discomfort or persecution because of it, bring it on, because I know You're my ultimate protection."

LYNDA: ✳I remember sitting in the backseat of my family's station wagon as a child, listening as my parents talked to the woman we'd brought with us that night to the church my dad pastored. She had prayed to receive Christ as her Savior. As she talked a lot about how much better her life was going to be, how God was going to take away all her troubles, Mom and Dad had to set her straight. I remember wondering if they would discourage her by explaining that she was really in harm's way now that she was a believer, but that she no longer had to live in fear because God would walk with her through it all. ✳

That's quite a deal: Bad stuff happens in life, but God protects us when we allow Him. Knowing that, we don't have to cower in some corner and be afraid to take risks.

REBECCA ✳ I once read about a survey conducted with men and women in their nineties. The question was, "If you had your life to live over again, what would you do differently?" One of the top three responses was that they would've taken more risks. One of my favorite movies is *Strictly Ballroom*, a film that focuses on ballroom dancing, in which the main theme is, "A life lived in fear is a life half-lived." If we allow fear to control us and refuse to take the risks God calls us to take, we will never live the SHE life or become an instrument God can use. ✳

In Matthew 14, Jesus instructed his disciple Peter to step out of the boat and walk on the water. Peter could have declined and remained status quo, but instead he chose to take the risk. He realized that through the risk Jesus could reveal His power in a whole new way. Peter settled the issue of his protection when he took that first step out of the boat. He discovered that as long as he kept his eyes on Jesus, he wouldn't sink.

You won't sink either if you keep your eyes on Jesus and do as He says. You'll have uncertain times and scary near misses, but those are a small price to pay for the greater accomplishments you'll be part of and the lessons you'll learn. You can choose to live a comfortable—and boring—life within the safety of the boat, or you can risk stepping out to see the exciting things Jesus has to teach you.

Be willing to take risks on those things (1) you feeling strongly about and (2) line up with God's truths. Don't let others talk you out of taking risks that meet these two criteria. Also, don't opt for the safety of inaction over the unknowns of risks. The SHE life is full of excitement and wise steps of faith. Don't resist them!

5. I must remain both offensive and defensive in protecting myself and those I love.

Lie: I am powerless in fighting danger.

Just as an intruder runs at the first sound of a siren, so does Satan when he sees we're wise to his tactics and prepared for his attacks. We don't want to be like those who get alarm systems only after an intruder has broken in. We want to be ready for the unpredictable.

> **LYNDA** ✳ I love the picture words in Matthew 12:29: "You can't enter a strong man's house and rob him without first tying him up. Only then can his house be robbed!"
>
> I picture myself, along with my husband, Dave, sitting at the door of our home, guarding us and our family from the intrusions of the enemy. We sit, not with a gun across our lap, but with an open Bible, learning its truths and passing on those values to our now-grown children—all the while refusing to give in to Satan's attempts to destroy our life and relationships.
>
> Many years ago, I heard a minister say that before our feet hit the floor every morning, we should pray Ephesians 6:14-17 over our family. I have done so in my own words ever since. In the car, at the

front door, over the phone—all my children know my prayer by heart and remind me when I forget:

"Lord, give us your helmet of salvation and your breastplate of righteousness. Gird our loins about with truth, and shod our feet with the preparation of the gospel of peace. Give us the sword of the Spirit, which is the Word of God, and the shield of faith to quench all the fiery darts of the evil one."

Every part of this armor is defensive, except for the sword, which is the Word of God—the truth we can base our life and battles upon. Recently my six-foot-one-inch college daughter stood at our front door where, like hundreds of times before, she waited for her mom to arm her through prayer and God's Word. We won't know except perhaps in eternity what those prayers have spared us from, but I have a feeling my children will be sharing this same prayer with their kids too. ✳

So dig in your heels and refuse to be taken off guard. Do what it takes to arm yourself both offensively and defensively.

6. God cares and He knows me by name.

Lie: If God really cared about me, He wouldn't let bad things happen to me.

As with Hagar, God not only cares about the situation you're going through, He calls you by name. He is the one reliable protector, and every aspect of your life hinges on Him. "This confidence [in God and His promise of heaven] is like a strong and trustworthy anchor for our souls."[10]

Picture yourself as a beautiful yacht that would be tossed about if it weren't for its secure anchor. God is your anchor and mine. Because of this, we are protected. We can know it. We can rest assured in it.

Here are two ways God provides His gentle protection. They'll work for you, guaranteed:

THROUGH HIS WORD

REBECCA ✳ There have been countless times when I'm struggling with something, and I'll read a particular Bible verse that hits the spot exactly. Many times tears have sprung to my eyes as I've seen how beautifully God encourages me and lets me know that He carries me through the good times and the bad. ✳

The Bible contains God's love letters to you, as well as His direction for decisions you need to make. It's essential to read it every day. Write in your journal or memorize verses that apply to what you're going through. Nothing ever has or ever will change God's truths.[11] You have His word on that!

THROUGH PRAYER

LYNDA ✳ God tells us in the Bible, "Look! Here I stand at the door and knock. If you hear me calling and open the door, I will come in, and we will share a meal as friends."[12] I have found that morning works best for me to spend time in prayer and in God's Word. Imagine doing breakfast with God! I can tell Him what's on my heart and find out what's on His. When I begin the morning that way and continue to shoot bullet prayers throughout the day or sing praise songs while I work or drive, I feel His protection, because my battles become His battles. ✳

God knows you'll feel most loved and protected by Him when you spend time in intimate conversations with Him. When the reality hits you that *God Himself* is listening to you, speaking His words to your heart and expressing His care, life doesn't get much better.

Set aside at least ten minutes every day to read the Bible and listen to what God has to say to you through His Word. Then spend at least ten minutes to pray and tell Him what's on your heart. As time goes on, you'll find yourself wanting to increase the time you spend with this One you've come to know through study and prayer. You won't want to go about your day without Him!

✳

Any security-system installer will tell you that most sales happen by word of mouth. Those who get a system see its value and convince others to do the same. Similarly, we can grow from needing to be only the *protected* to also being a *protector*. In addition to needing to

be protected, each of us will be assigned the protection of someone
else sometime in life. Whether for children or parents or friends, at
times we'll need to step in to the position of one who guards or protects. When we do, we'll understand how to both protect and let go
because God has modeled those for us.

LYNDA ✳ My greatest role as a protector started when I became a
mom, especially when I became a single mom. Instead of sharing my
role with a dependable protector-husband, I had to do it alone. In June,
after my kids and I moved to Colorado for my job at Focus on the Family,
I had to put my children on a plane to visit their dad for a whole month. I
hadn't been away from them for longer than a week before that time,
and they were going back to a less than ideal situation. So I began to
grieve. I felt fearful, worried, and angry—all at the same time. I cried
constantly and had difficulty doing my work. Even at my strong moments of trusting God, I found myself wondering, *Will they be okay?*

One week and one day after they left, I awoke and as I dressed for
church, I prayed another time for them. As I did, God clearly spoke to my
heart the word *Jochebed.* I'd never heard the word before, but in my
emotional, desperate state of mind, I didn't stop to ask questions. I
searched for the word in my Bible concordance. Eventually I found
Jochebed, Moses' mother. I read how she "kept him hidden for three
months. But when she could no longer hide him" from Pharaoh's threats,
she released him among the reeds along the banks of the Nile River.[13]

Then I realized that Jochebed was just like me! Her role as protector had been interrupted. She had to release her tiny baby physically to
the danger of the waters, spiritually to the possibility that he'd choose a
godless life over his Jewish heritage, and emotionally to whom he'd grow
up calling Mom. I needed to do the same. I had to do all I could to hide my
children from danger, and then I had to do all I could to turn them over to
God to protect them physically, spiritually, and emotionally.

I met Moses' mother more than ten years ago, and I've been
"Jochebedding" them ever since. Whether those we love and need to
protect get behind the wheel of a car or grow old or take off for college
or get their heart broken by a first love, we must learn to release them
and then stand back and let God be their Protector.

With the help God offers, we can grow from being unprotected to finding safety in His protection and extending that protection to other people in our life. Even if someone left you or lied to you or let you down when they should have kept you safe. Even if you still hurt or struggle to trust. God knows your unprotected past and present, and He wants to cover you under the shadow of His wings and offer you an exciting, confident way forward under His protection. Go ahead! Try it! There's no safer place to be. ✳

✳ **SHEism** ✳ A truly protected SHE finds her protection in God and through His arms of family and community, and the wisdom He provides.

Additional Resources:

Philip Yancey, **Disappointment with God** (Grand Rapids, Mich.: Zondervan, 1988)

Judith Couchman, **The Shadow of His Hand** (Colorado Springs: Waterbrook Press, 2002)

Kari West, **Dare to Trust, Dare to Hope Again** (Colorado Springs: Cook Communications Ministries, 2001)

Chuck Swindoll, **Hope Again: When Life Hurts and Dreams Fade** (Nashville: Word Publishers, 1996)

"Intimacy connotes familiarity and closeness. It involves our deepest nature, and it is marked by a warm friendship developed through long association. In order for us to become intimate with another, we must find in him a true confidant—one in whom we can safely confide our secrets."

Cynthia Heald *Intimacy with God* [1]

"Friendship with God is reserved for those who reverence him. With them alone he shares the secrets of his promises."

Psalm 25:14, TLB

Chapter 3

Intimate: Unraveling the Lone-Ranger Mentality

REBECCA ✳ I received this e-mail from a fifteen-year-old girl:

I've been through a lot in my life: seven years of sexual abuse at the hands of my father, the death of my grandfather, and the recent death of my best friend. I've been hurt and abandoned by almost everyone who says they care. It's hard, so I struggle with the issue of God's love all the time. When I feel myself getting closer to God in worship, I get so scared and panicked that I have to leave because my life has told me that when you get close to someone you get hurt. ✳

It's no surprise that this girl has such a tough time letting people in. Her safety on all kinds of levels has been compromised over and over throughout her young life. The only way she knows to protect her heart from more pain is to keep it slammed shut and dead-bolted—and who can blame her? As a result, even her ability to trust God has been damaged. Life has taught her that being close to others will lead to hurt.

That brings us to the second characteristic of a **S**afe SHE: SHE grows to understand the safety of genuine intimacy.

Before reading on, take a few minutes and consider how well you can relate to this girl. Granted, you may not have suffered abuse or feelings of abandonment. But everyone at some time or other knows what it feels like to be hurt by someone else. For others of you, this young girl's story hits far too close to home. Can you answer yes to any of the following questions?

* Do you resist getting close to others for fear of being hurt?

* Do you mistrust God because of the ways people have let you down?

* Do you feel that no one understands the real you?

* Do you often fight feelings of loneliness?

* Is intimacy a foreign concept to you?

Intimacy: The Good, the Bad, and the Ugly

We hear about intimacy all the time—how fulfilled we are when we find it and how empty we are when we don't. Women, especially, seek intimacy and even tend to allow their "intimate" relationships to define them in much the same way that men often feel defined by their vocations.

Intimate is a word used to describe a cozy table in the corner of a restaurant, a deep conversation between friends, a sexual act between lovers, and a personal relationship with God. Some say intimacy is emotional; others keep it strictly physical. Some say it's all in the head; others say it's found in bed. One word, lots of perspectives.

The word *intimate* isn't in the Bible, so we can't go there to settle the issue of its real meaning. In this chapter, we'd like to define intimacy as "the ability to connect deeply with someone." This connection can happen on many fronts: emotional, physical, spiritual, romantic, and platonic.

Intimacy is also complex. We want it because we hope it means we'll feel cared for and secure. We want to be understood and loved completely. We hope it will mean no more loneliness. But there's another side to it that we're not so fond of.

Intimacy engages the deepest parts of who we are; it requires *depth*. The best relationships get to the bottom of the deep-down, nitty-gritty details that make up our thoughts, faults, shortcomings, fears, and shame, as well as all our more positive qualities. Frankly, that can be frightening. After all, being known—*truly* known—means that the most private and sometimes embarrassing parts of who we are, the worst of all our junk, become apparent to someone else. And that someone else has the power to use that junk against us. Our secrets are out; our biggest and baddest self is uncovered and laid bare. It's exposure. And it's scary.

> Intimacy is the ability to connect deeply with someone.

LYNDA ❊ Even as a child, I recognized the vulnerability that bit at the heels of intimacy. At the edge of a woods behind my family's home, I spent a lot of time sitting on a gate post, pretending, imagining, and dreaming about my life: what I wanted to be, who I would marry, how I would impact the world, when I would overcome some of my weaknesses and insecurities. But even the wildest of my imaginations took place in silence. I didn't dare speak aloud about those things closest to my heart and least known to others. I remember feeling fearful that if someone heard my grandiose plans, they might laugh, or worse yet, try to destroy them. So as days turned into months, I grew more and more comfortable with choosing safety over intimacy and isolation over letting someone else in. ❊

Obviously we wouldn't feel safe letting someone know the worst—or even the best—about us unless we were sure those things wouldn't be reasons for that person to betray us or run from us. That person must prove to be trustworthy and safe. So intimacy also demands *width*—it grows in the midst of and through the many shared conversations and activities that are part of the memory box of a devoted and lasting friendship.

An additional test of time takes place that makes or breaks any relationship—time to experience many different situations, environments, joys, and stresses together. Intimacy involves *length*—it develops over a sustained period or season of life.

Because intimacy involves depth, width, and length, it includes the best and the worst—the good, the bad, and the ugly. We want it but we don't. . . . But we really do.

A study entitled "Americans Identify What They Want out of Life," which researcher George Barna conducted in 2000, reported the following:

✷ Three-quarters of the adult population said that having close personal friendships is a top priority.

✷ Slightly fewer Americans (seven out of ten) indicated that having a close personal relationship with God is a top priority.

✷ Thirty percent of Americans are "trying to find a few good friends."[2]

In response to our cry for intimacy, magazines line the racks with headlines about it, TV sitcoms such as *Friends* have based their popularity on this theme, and pastors teach about its importance.

REBECCA AND LYNDA ✷ We constantly hear from women like the one mentioned at the beginning of this chapter who are crying out for intimacy with someone—anyone—who will care about their deepest longings. We see evidence of a lack of intimacy with people as well as with God. But we believe that by learning to connect deeply with God, we can learn to connect deeply with others, too. In fact, intimacy in its fullest form cannot happen between people until those people first experience depth with God. ✷

God-Intimacy

God wants a personal relationship with you. Is your heart moved when you think about that? The God of the universe created you and knows all about you—and He pulled out all the stops and went to the greatest lengths possible to invite you into the safety of His love. He knows it all—your weaknesses as well as your strengths; your good choices as well as your bad; your confident places as well as your insecure ones. And He's been pursuing you every moment of your life.[3]

You can know *about* God without really *knowing* Him. But what He offers you is a wonderful gift: intimacy with Him. In every event between Genesis and Revelation, yesterday and someday, God has been seeking a deep, personal relationship with every one of His kids. Theologian A. W. Tozer writes:

> *Deep inside every human being there is a private sanctum, a secret place where only God can dwell. He has planted something of Himself (eternity) in every human breast . . . a divinely implanted sense of purpose, which nothing or no one but God can satisfy.*[4]

But most of us either don't know it's possible to have a personal relationship with God or fail to grasp the utter necessity of this life-changing truth. Or we may forgo this closeness with God because our heavenly-Father image has been tainted by the image we've developed of our earthly father, and we have trouble seeing God-intimacy as an inviting possibility. Joseph Stowell, author and president of Moody Bible Institute, says that the absence of intimacy with God is like channel surfing life as we look for something to hold our attention. We grow accustomed to living at a distance from God and eventually believe that this kind of divine closeness isn't what it's cracked up to be. Intimacy with God—or the absence of it—drives our intimacy with life.

LYNDA ✳ A pastor's wife approached me after she'd heard me speak about God-intimacy at a retreat. With tears in her eyes, she said, "I don't know how to be intimate with Jesus. I only know how to check the boxes when I pray and read the Bible. But intimacy? I just don't know how."

Author, pastor, and theologian Calvin Miller calls intimacy *inwardness*, and he also points out how we tend to substitute lots of other things when we don't find it: "When God does not fill the vacuum, a host of consuming appetites swarm through our better intentions."[5]

God-intimacy: We're made for it and we suffer in many ways
when we don't find it. Its absence leaves a void, a vacancy, a hole in our
heart that can never be filled with anything or anyone else. Further, this
absence actually *hinders* our search for closeness with others. ✳

People-Intimacy

God Himself created us for people-intimacy, which is the ability to
connect with others on a deep level. He said, "It is not good for the
man to be alone. I will make a companion who will help him."[6]

We need each other. But true people-intimacy has been the exception since shortly after God created us. After Adam and Eve first
sinned, God informed Eve, "Though your desire will be for your husband, he will be your master."[7] Not only did sin separate them (and
us) from God, it also continues to wreak havoc in our relationships
with each other.

REBECCA ✳ One brilliant, mid-September Saturday I went to a
beautiful park to write. The day couldn't have been more perfect. White,
fluffy clouds floated through the sky and a gentle breeze blew across my
face. Expecting the park to be packed, I was surprised to notice that the
only people I saw were a few runners on the path and boys playing football in the playground area. I wondered where everyone was and decided
parents must have been doing their own thing while the kids did theirs. I
felt a twinge of sadness that the park wasn't filled with families and
friends spending time together, playing, laughing, eating, and talking. It
spoke to me about the lack of community in our society today. ✳

Somewhere we have forgotten the importance of depth and
time spent in relationships. Respected psychologist Larry Crabb
wrote about this failure to find true people-intimacy:

*Most people go through their entire life never speaking words to
another human being that come out of what is deepest within them,
and most people never hear words that reach all the way into the
deep place we call the soul. But we all have the power to relate to*

*people in such a way that we can say, "There's something within
me—and something within you—that, if known, explored,
discovered, touched, released, could move you toward the vision and
maturity God has for you, whether anything in your circumstances
changes or not."*[8]

Today the intimacy-replacing "enmity" God predicted between
people causes half of all first marriages and 60 percent of second marriages to end in divorce, with a median duration of less than eight
years for both. And many of the ones that stay intact never find the
true intimacy desired.[9]

So what are the culprits that prevent and destroy this much-
needed, much-wanted intimacy that God designed us to have? Here
are a few we came up with:

* Isolation   * Transience   * Family breakdown

* Poor role models * Selfishness   * Misplaced priorities

* Cultural lies   * Cultural focus   * Shame
                       on independence

* Packed schedules

When we allow these and other things to prevent or destroy our
important relationships, we often find damaging substitutes to meet
our need for companionship. Psychologists call those substitutes false
intimacies. They keep us from connecting deeply with God and others
and stifle our growth as an individual. Those hurts can lead to a
lone-ranger mentality, in which we live as if it's us—and us only—
against the world. Because our heart feels unsafe, we behave defensively or possessively toward others and become jealous and distrust-
ful. We push others away and often complete the self-fulfilling
prophesy of rejection, which continues the damaging cycle.

Check Your Intimacy Quotient

Love is a natural part of any intimate relationship. The specific experience of love, however, is unique for each of us. Love relationships

vary, because people have had different experiences with love during early childhood. Just as babies need secure parental attachment that provides a solid emotional base from which to explore the world, so also adults need love relationships to gain the sense of confidence and self-worth that enables them to develop their potential and use their creative talents to the fullest. By examining the three major styles[10] of love relationships that develop between infants and their parents, we can better understand why as adults we do or do not make intimate attachments of our own. Which of the following best describes your feelings?

1. I find it relatively easy to get close to God and others and am comfortable depending on them and having them depend on me. I don't often worry about being abandoned or about someone getting too close to me.

2. I am somewhat uncomfortable being close to God and others and find it difficult to trust and to allow myself to depend on them. I am nervous when anyone gets too close, and often God and others want me to be more intimate than I am comfortable with.

3. I find that others are reluctant to get as close as I would like and often worry that others don't really love me or won't want to stay with me. My desire to be merged or swallowed up in a relationship with someone causes smothered feelings, which typically scares that person away.

If number 1 above describes your feelings, we're going to call you a *receiver* of intimacy. You have a secure style of attachment to other people. You trust people you love and see yourself as worthy of being loved. You find it easy to get close to others and feel comfortable relying on those people. You don't worry about being abandoned or having someone demand too much depth and vulnerability from you. Peers find you confident, likeable, and open. You probably describe your parents as caring and responsive.

A number 2 choice would make you a *resister* of intimacy. When someone tries to get close to you, you feel uncomfortable. You find it hard to trust another person completely and don't like to be dependent. You may claim not to believe in romantic love or the need for it, as if trying to compensate for deep insecurities. Others describe you as relatively defensive. You probably describe your parents as hostile indifferent, cold, or rejecting.

Finally, if you related to number 3, you could be called a *repeller* of intimacy. You often worry that other people don't truly love you and won't stay with you for long. Your desire to get really close sometimes scares other people away. If you're single, you might find yourself preoccupied with finding "real" love, constantly falling in and out of relationships, but true love has eluded you. If you are married, you have trouble being your own person or feeling secure within your marriage. As a repeller, you often fail to find true friends, and confidence in yourself is characterized by emotional extremes and self-doubts. Peers could describe you as self-conscious, insecure, and preoccupied with relationship issues. You probably describe your parents in both positive and negative terms, suggesting inconsistent parenting.

Psychologists say that the relationship style a person develops tends to endure.[11] But God says something else. He's been in the healing business for thousands of years, and He can make change happen for you or someone you love.[12] There's no hurt He can't heal and no chain He can't break.

Meaningful and lasting connections with God and others are vital parts of being a healthy person. If you've realized you're a resister or repeller of intimacy, we hope this chapter sheds light on becoming a receiver.

✳ Do you want greater understanding and connection with those closest to you?

✳ Do you want to move past shallow friendships and into meaningful ones?

✳ Do you want a closer marriage and a healthier connection with your kids?

✳ Do you want to know God deeply?

✳ Do you want to stop acting as if everything's okay, and be able to be gut-level honest with people instead?

Here's an example of two women who understood the safety of opening their heart and knowing—and being known by—Jesus.

Mary and Mary: Intimacy Received (Mark 15–16; Luke 10; John 11–12)

Mary of Bethany and Mary of Magdala—two Marys from the Bible, two intimacy receivers.

Mary of Bethany housed Him. Mary of Magdala depended on Him for her very life. They came from different locations and backgrounds, but one thing brought them together—their love for Jesus. Their encounters with Him varied, as did His impact on each of them. But in Him they both found a safe place for the deepest needs of their hearts. Spending time with Him brought wholeness and wisdom for life, including intimacy with others. Let's look at their stories.

Mary of Bethany

Bethany was a town just two miles from Jerusalem. When Jesus passed through Bethany, He often stayed at Mary's home, where she lived with her brother, Lazarus, and her sister, Martha. The biblical account of her story shows how much she valued her time with Jesus, which was even more rare considering the lowly status of women in her day and culture. Tradition tells us that one of the prayers Jewish men prayed every morning was, "Thank you, God, that you did not make me a slave, nor a heathen, nor a woman." But Jesus introduced a new respect for women, and Mary found ways to be with Him often. She appears in three major scenes alongside Jesus. Each gives a glimpse of her closeness to Him.

We first meet Mary in her home when Jesus came to visit.[13] While Martha busied herself in the kitchen preparing food for their guest, Mary sat at His feet and hung on His every word. She learned the truths He taught. His truths became her life's purpose. When Martha complained that Mary wasn't helping in the kitchen, Jesus described the difference between a *doing* relationship with Him and an *intimate* one. "My dear Martha, you are so upset over all these details! There is really only one thing worth being concerned about. Mary has discovered it—and I won't take it away from her."[14]

We read about Mary again in John 11, after her brother, Lazarus, died.[15] When Lazarus had grown ill, Mary and Martha sent for Jesus, but He delayed coming in order to show His glory. Lazarus had died by the time Jesus finally arrived. Mary dropped to her familiar place—down at His feet—and poured out her heart in full honesty: "Lord, if you had been here, my brother would not have died."[16] Jesus wept with Mary, and then He went to raise Lazarus from the dead. Jesus' delay gave Mary the opportunity to know His character and power on a deeper level.

Before we move to our third encounter with Mary of Bethany, one can't help but wonder what happened between the verses of Scripture. Did Mary walk to the marketplace one day and overhear soldiers saying that they would crucify Jesus? Did she run back across the cobblestones to her home and touch the place where He always sat and she always listened? Did she glance at the bed where her now-alive and healed brother slept? Did her heart ache at the possibility that her time with Jesus was coming to an end? How much did she know about what Jesus would endure?

What we *do* know is that six days before Jesus' death, Jesus accompanied His disciples to a dinner at the home of Simon the leper, the father of Judas Iscariot.[17] As they reclined at the table, talking—maybe about Simon's healing or Lazarus's coming back from the dead—the door opened, and Mary made her third appearance that the Bible records. A hush might have fallen over the room as she moved across the floor and bowed, once again, at Jesus' feet. She held a pint of pure nard, an expensive perfume made from a rare Himalayan plant and perhaps the most valuable thing she owned. With this costly possession, she anointed Jesus, performing the greatest act of honor a commoner could bestow on royalty. She poured it on His feet, despite objections that she was wasting it instead of selling it and giving the money to the poor. Jesus' defense was simple, "You will always have the poor among you, but I will not be here with you much longer."[18] And so the house was filled with the fragrance of the perfume from someone who'd become an intimacy receiver at Jesus' feet.

Mary of Magdala

Magdala was a town on the western shore of the Sea of Galilee. It was in that region that Mary of Magdala met Jesus, when He cast seven demons out of her.[19] We don't know the nature of those demons, but we do know the impact the deliverance had on Mary's life. Mary left Magdala—and stuck close to Him for the remainder of His time on earth. Her name and her well-documented place alongside Jesus appear many times in the Gospels.

It would come as no surprise if we knew that Mary's desire to be with Jesus was partly because she remembered how tormented her life had been without Him. She knew firsthand the bondage and pain that evil caused, and she knew the freedom and safety she had found with Jesus. To stay close to Him would mean she'd have a defense against Satan's future attacks.

It's apparent from her story that she cherished her relationship with Jesus. It was about intimacy. She expressed her love and gratitude. She stayed near Him, listening to His voice, seeing compassion in His eyes, and absorbing His teaching. She was there till the end. She followed Him when He carried the cross toward Calvary. She surely cried as she watched Him being tortured.[20]

Early on resurrection morning, the streets were quiet. Mary joined a group of other women on their way to Jesus' grave to finish embalming His body.[21] They had stopped their work Friday night because the Sabbath observance had begun. Then it was time to complete her last act of adoration for Jesus by anointing His body with embalming oil, and she heard His voice call her by name: "Mary!" He said.[22]

It's one thing to realize that we get to know Jesus; it's quite another to realize that we get to be known by Him too. He knows us and calls us by name. Mary's response reflected her similar familiarity: *Rabboni*, she called him, an intimate word for "teacher" in Aramaic, the language Jesus had used when He talked with her. At that moment, Mary of Magdala became the first witness of the most important truth of salvation: Jesus' resurrection. Then Jesus told her not to touch Him, but to go and tell the others that He was alive.[23]

Mary. Her intimacy with her Lord brought her the gift of being the first not only to witness the Resurrection but to announce it to the others also. The intimate friendship Mary had known with Jesus was complete, but her spiritual journey had just begun.

So had ours. Seven weeks later on the Day of Pentecost, the Holy Spirit fell on those who followed Christ. Although Mary's name is not mentioned as one of those present, scholars tell us she was probably there. That same Holy Spirit would show Mary and all believers the way to daily intimacy with the risen Lord.

Intimacy and You

Both Marys understood intimacy with God as well as intimacy with others. Mary of Magdala had a beautiful love and reverence for Jesus, caring for His needs even to the end, but she also had friendships with women and men. In nearly every biblical account that we read of her, she is described as being with a group of people. They experienced together the life-changing events of Jesus' last days. She didn't shy away from community and relationships. She was not a lone ranger.

We can best love others when we know God's love.

LYNDA ✳ Whether they knew they were doing it or not, my children have made me aware of the correlation between intimacy with God and intimacy with others. They've said to me more than once when I've been grumpy or distant, "Mom, don't you need to go upstairs and spend some time with God?" ✳

We learn how to love by spending time with the God of love. We learn how to relate to others by learning God's way of relating. When we find security in God, we're free to love others without fear. We no longer need to take, take, take from them in a draining or codependent fashion to become whole, because we're already whole in Christ. Instead, we share from the overflow of our intimacy with God into our intimacy with others.

> We learn how to love by spending time with the God of love.

Again, let's go to the root of the lies we often fall for—lies that destroy our deep relationships both with God and with people.

❋ *SHE Lives the Truth* ❋

1. If I'm too busy to cultivate intimacy with God, I'm too busy.

Lie: I don't have time to cultivate intimacy with God.

It takes less time to cultivate and enjoy the results of spiritual intimacy than it does to deal with the consequences of resisting or repelling it. The intimacy Mary of Magdala and Mary of Bethany found grew out of very natural, day-to-day time spent with Jesus. It's as simple as that. Mary of Bethany sat constantly at His feet, regardless of whether things were good (as when she was listening to Him in their home) or bad (as when her brother died). She knelt before Him—in all her circumstances. Closeness also characterized Mary of Magdala's relationship with Jesus. She followed Him around wherever He went. He knew her well, and she had come to know Him too. Both Marys took the time for intimacy with Jesus, and by doing so avoided the time it would have taken to figure out and handle life on their own.

Here are a few tools for igniting and sustaining intimacy with your Lord:

REGULAR PRAYER

Time spent with Jesus involves talking to Him about the good times as well as the bad. It requires two-way communication: telling Him what's on your heart and listening to what's on His. Lynda's favorite time for talking to Him is in the morning. Rebecca's special time with Jesus is much later in the day.

> **REBECCA** ❋ Kind of like wanting to talk on the phone to my best friend about something that has happened during my day, when I'm struggling to find strength and proper perspective amidst a grueling schedule on the road, I often shoot up bullet prayers to God and ask Him for help. I also find that being honest with friends about my struggles and asking them to pray for me and support me really empowers my life. Someone I know keeps several praying friends informed of her

speaking schedule. She says she never takes the stage without knowing that at least three people are lifting her up before God. ✳

REGULAR BIBLE READING

The Bible contains God's words for our lives. We can know Him
better through knowing the Bible.

Suggestions for Bible Reading:

✳ Select a read-through-the-Bible-in-a-year version.

✳ Read devotional books daily, but don't allow this to make up your
entire spiritual diet. Make sure you read the actual Bible every
day too.

✳ Memorize Scriptures, which reinforce the truths and counteract
the lies.

✳ Alter your techniques of reading. If the same time of day gets boring to you, add a noontime or bedtime Bible reading. You could try
reading your Bible on your knees to stay focused.

SYSTEMATIC STUDY

We all love to read love letters. We feel comforted when we get cards
of encouragement or hope when we're in hard places. We seek out
guidance that will show us how to deal with life's challenges. God's
Word is all of this and more. In black and white (and sometimes even
red) letters, we can read His message of love, encouragement, hope,
and direction. Those words were written for you.

Use some resources such as a concordance and commentaries
to study the details of Scripture.

TIME TO LEARN WITH OTHERS

Spend time with people who want to know God. *Fellowship* is a word
used to describe quality time spent with others who want to know
God too. Fellowship can happen with a trusted friend or with total
strangers. The key is knowing Jesus. One caution, however: Don't

spend *all* your time with other Christians. The purpose of fellowship is to help you grow in wisdom and faith. The purpose of that growth is to take it out to a lost and dying world and tell others about this God you're getting to know so well in the quiet places of prayer, study, and fellowship. Church, Bible studies, small groups, and retreats provide settings for discovering that fellowship.

> **LYNDA** ✳ I became involved in a Bible study with a few other young moms after my first child was born. We studied the book of Matthew, which gave me my first chance to study in depth and dig details out of Scripture. That experience set the stage for my personal Bible study in the years to come. ✳

2. God is a Father to the fatherless.

Lie: My terrible relationship with my earthly father will always keep me from a good relationship with God.

> **LYNDA** ✳ I mentored a pastor's wife, Amy, who had suffered extreme abuse at the hands of her father. I met with her once a week, and we studied the book *A God to Call Father.*[24] When we began, I helped her visibly place her father and her mother, whom she blamed for allowing the things to happen, on a shelf while we listened to what God had to say to Amy herself. This helped her differentiate between Father God and earthly father. As we moved along, we tackled different aspects of the hard things she had dealt with. ✳

Amy is not alone in her lack of a positive father figure. Forty percent of American children live in homes without their father. Fatherlessness is one of the most urgent problems in America today.[25]

Here's an interesting project for the year. Do a word study from the Bible, looking up in a concordance every verse that contains the word *father*. Keep a chart of the characteristics that emerge (compassionate, forgiving, faithful, etc.). When necessary, find Hebrew and Greek meanings in the back of the concordance. Then as you pray, ask God to become to you the qualities you read about in His Word. Keep track of ways He answers your prayers.

3. When I find intimacy with God, He can show me how to find intimacy with others, too.

Lie: I'm incapable of experiencing intimacy with others.

Once again, it is the truth of God's Scripture that shows us how to live our life. We start trusting God by praying and reading His Word. We realize that He will protect and guide us. So while He's keeping us safe, we let Him guide us to trust others, too. We discover that the more we step toward trusting others, the more we invite them to share the joy of intimacy. The same is true for communicating: As we learn to communicate with God, He shows us His truths about communicating with others. He shows us how to listen, for example. People long to be heard. It's been said that the reason there are so many counselors and psychologists is because people have forgotten how to really listen. By listening, we invite the closeness of others.

In his book *Secrets to Lasting Love*, author Gary Smalley writes that intimacy with people happens as a result of a journey through five progressively deepening levels of communication: (1) clichés; (2) facts; (3) opinions, concerns, and expectations; (4) feelings; and (5) needs. As we talk God and enter a more personal relationship with Him, our level of vulnerability will deepen in similar ways.[26] Spend time with that special person . . . washing dishes, throwing a ball, riding together in the car. Togetherness unifies, especially in informal situations. Ask your friend or spouse deep, probing questions about who they are, what their dreams are, and what God is teaching them. Then listen to what they say.

Do special things for that person, such as sending flowers or a card. Share a devotion or prayer time together. It works wonders in a marriage!

Read through Proverbs. Note all the verses that talk about relationships with others. What are they asking of you?

Do another word search in the Bible. Find out about words like *friendship* or *listening*. Ask God to help you treat others more like He treats us in these areas.

✳

If you aim first for intimacy with God, He'll open the door to discovering wonderful relationships with others.

REBECCA ✳ I have a friend named Tanya. Life has been tough for this nineteen-year-old, who has experienced abuse, a dysfunctional family, suicidal tendencies, and more. When I first met her she was a scarred, scared, hurting young woman who was so crippled by her emotional pain that she couldn't relate well to God or people. Now she is a radiant, whole, God-loving woman who enjoys closeness with her Savior, and because of this, with others. Tanya recently shared these words with me:

> Tonight I got on my face before God. I prayed, and I sat in silence. I was reading and listening to what God was saying to me. "Therefore I am now going to allure her; I will lead her into the desert and speak tenderly to her. There I will give her back her vineyards, and will make the Valley of Achor a door of hope. There she will sing as in the days of her youth, as in the day she came up out of Egypt" [Hosea 2:14-15].
>
> Achor means "trouble." God will make the valley of trouble a door of hope. When I realize that God is all I need and God is all I want, then He can give me back my vineyards and all the other vineyards that I want.
>
> However, if I don't understand that God is all I need, those other things will only be distractions to me. What I really want is for Him to show Himself to me and speak to me in ways that He never has before. And I want to show Him how much I love Him.

Tanya has become intimate with God, which has helped her grow in intimacy with others. Out of that she has found safety. She trusts the God she has come to know, who teaches her how to trust—and become intimate with—others. ✳

✳ **SHEism** ✳ A truly intimate SHE is a woman who finds intimacy with God, and then allows Him to guide her toward finding safe intimacy with others.

Additional Resources:

Lynda Hunter Bjorklund, **The Hungry Heart** (Wheaton, Ill.: Tyndale House Publishers, 2004)

Richard Foster, **The Celebration of Discipline** (San Francisco: Harper SanFrancisco, 1988)

Gary Smalley, **Secrets to Lasting Love** (New York: Simon and Schuster, 2000)

Gary Chapman, **The Five Love Languages: How to Express Heartfelt Commitment to Your Mate** (Chicago: Northfield Publishing Co., 1992)

"In my mind, the most feminine woman is one with an eye and ear for others and a heart for God."

Emily Barnes[1]

"You should be known for . . . a gentle and quiet spirit, which is so precious to God."

1 Peter 3:4

Chapter 4

Feminine: The New Femininity

LYNDA ❊ During my fourteen years as a single mom of three, I daily moved mountains to make life work. Like other parents raising kids on their own, I had to do it all. When traveling became necessary, one of my added tasks was to find someone—or someones—to don the many hats I wore while I was away. I got really good at achieving things people noticed and feminists applauded—including earning my doctorate, which I began when my children were five, three, and one. I became really good at making schedules work. I got really good at persevering through obstacles.

I got really bad, however, at staying soft and feminine. I traded patience for protectiveness, compassion for convenience, and sensitivity for schedules. When my children got sick, unless they were throwing up or burning up, I pushed them to keep to their regular routine. After all, there wasn't time for illness in my rigid plans. As a result, they rarely missed school, but they did miss out on some tender parts of my love. One morning as I prepared to go to the zoo with Ashley's kindergarten class, she said, "Mom, laugh and tell jokes today. Laugh and tell jokes." Ashley said this three times before I realized she was asking to see the softer, less businesslike, more fun side of me. But home wasn't the only place my "fun" side was lacking.

I also had gotten really bad about working alongside others and under someone else's leadership. In a healthy marriage, the husband and wife labor together as a united front toward the same goal. Both good marriages and good working conditions require a competent leader and allow everyone under that leader the freedom to give input. I didn't have a husband to bounce things off of and to work with toward a common goal. Add to that the fact that I didn't really have personal contact with a boss during my postgrad work and university teaching, and the result was life that seemed to proceed on its own.

So did I. I did as I pleased and answered to no one but God and myself. I grew harsh and black-and-white and often judgmental. I became extremely regimented and independent and always focused on the bottom line. I also worked extra hard and took on seemingly impossible challenges to prove my worth and competence. And I especially liked having others rate me as a "Superwoman" or "Wondermom."

After I finished teaching at the university and got real jobs with real bosses—all men—I struggled with being under their authority. After all, I had effectively run a "company" of four for so many years; it was natural that I had trouble accepting any role that wasn't the one in command. Many times I quietly decided that I could do the job better, and even when I complied outwardly, inwardly I held a grudge. I gave little thought to needing other people or polishing my skills for working effectively with them. And in the midst of it all, I didn't even realize the impact culture had had on the way I did life and measured achievement.

About this time of my crisis in femininity, authors Gary Smalley and John Trent released a book called *The Two Sides of Love*,[2] which described a lot of what I was experiencing. In that book, Smalley and Trent defined four personality types that they illustrated as the lion, the beaver, the otter, and the golden retriever.

The authors pointed out that while some character qualities

come naturally to certain personality types, others have to be built in. The otter and the golden retriever would have no trouble with compassion, grace, and mercy, but they might have a tendency to be taken advantage of by others. Lions and beavers, on the other hand, organize life to a T and are viewed as being ultracapable, but their love can become harsh and inflexible. While organization comes easily to them, they have to work hard to find tenderness in their relationships. In other words, otters and retrievers need to develop more the hard side of their love, while lions and beavers need to grow a softness. ✳

REBECCA AND LYNDA ✳ We believe that the key to our own femininity is found in a similar kind of balance. What Smalley and Trent call the need to develop both hard and soft sides, we call the need to be "tough but tender." Hang in there with us as we explain. ✳

The Feminine "Mistake"

In 1963, Betty Friedan published her now-famous book called *The Feminine Mystique*, which officially launched the feminist movement. She insisted that women of her day felt unhappy and stifled. From their roles as a wife and mom, they were asking, "Is this all?" and making comments such as

✳ "I feel empty somehow, incomplete."

✳ "I feel as if I don't exist."

✳ "I feel like crying for no reason."

Friedan called this rash of discontentment among wives and moms "the problem that has no name." She wrote, "The problem that has no name is simply the fact that American women are kept from growing to their full human capacities."[3]

Why did Friedan's view strike such a nerve with women? Let's backtrack a bit to see how history had made us ripe for change.

After the stock market crashed in 1929, the U.S. Supreme Court ruled to adopt a minimum-wage law for women in response to massive labor strikes. Then World War II arrived on America's doorstep in 1941, sending women to work to support the country. Despite their contributions to the economy during that time, women's career opportunities largely remained limited once the conflict was over.

By the 1960s, more women were going to college than ever before, yet women who remained at home with their family received little respect, and those who went into the workplace were treated as inferior to men.

That's why our culture embraced Betty Friedan's 1963 book.

However, while history was ready for a change where women were concerned, the church didn't help guide this change in a godly, moral direction. Once we realized the course feminism was taking, our window of opportunity had closed to only a crack. As Christians, we somehow missed our chance to impact the development of modern feminism. Author Diane Passno writes, "Since the church has been quiet on the issue, or has subordinated itself to the movement, our cultural pendulum has now swung completely to the secular extreme."[4]

By the 1970s, abortion became legal and the Equal Rights Amendment became law. Radical feminists infiltrated college campuses with women's studies and the philosophy that, except for physical variations, there were no differences between men and women. That view kicked off years of gender confusion and a boom in "anti-men" attitudes, blaming the entire sex for holding women back and suppressing our potential. Passno describes these issues, which "usually pose women as the victims of white, oppressive males, and the culture as a hotbed of gender discrimination, sexual harassment, and misogyny."[5] As a result, feminism has affected and confused women, men, and children.

The dictionary defines feminism as "the theory of the political, economic, and social equality of the sexes."[6] It began for some solid reasons and desires to change gross injustices for women such as the inability to vote. To a large extent, however, feminism has grown to be selfish in nature and is concerned more with the wants and needs of the individual than of the whole, thus distorting its positive potential. The focus of ultrafeminism is not the good of humanity or even the good of the average American woman.

Friedan drew many of her discontentment conclusions from magazine articles she observed in her day. Four decades passed, giving women space to find our own answers and time to achieve more of the goals we were thought to have missed out on. In the late 1990s, Danielle Crittenden did a follow-up study. She examined thirty years' worth of back issues of *Mademoiselle, Glamour, Vogue, Redbook, Cosmopolitan,* and *McCalls* magazines. Many circumstances had changed for women in those thirty years; many rights had been achieved. But had these social transformations made women more content? Had these changes brought more happiness and fulfillment?

Crittenden says no. She wrote, "It's a stark descent from the ebullience and optimism of the dawning of the modern women's movement in the early 1970s to the disappointment and bitterness you see in these publications today."[7] Neither a woman's right to choose nor the equal rights she achieved through Congress brought the utopia women had searched for.

Crittenden concludes that the modern problem with no name is the reverse of the old problem: "While we now recognize that women are human, we blind ourselves to the fact that we are also women . . . we suffer every bit as much when cut off from those aspects of life that are distinctly and uniquely female."[8]

Feminism Fallout

How has feminism affected you as an individual? Let's take a look at some societal impacts of feminism and how they might affect your everyday life as a citizen:

Feminism's inconsistencies and politically correct language have confused the issues and dulled society's sense of right and wrong.

Unborn babies are called "fetuses" or "blobs" to justify abortion.

Feminism has promoted a self-centered mentality.

In droves, women are leaving their marriage and God-given responsibilities and focusing, instead, on the grass-is-greener promise touted by culture.

Feminism has created a victim mentality, which shifts the blame and negates accountability.

As our society has grown more and more litigious, we as citizens have started taking less responsibility for our own mistakes.

Feminism has confused gender roles, leaving both women and men insecure in relating to each other.

Women complain, "Chivalry is dead." Men complain, "I open the door for her—she says she can do it herself; I don't open it—she says I'm rude and don't treat her right. What *does* she want?"

Feminism has painted biblical standards of morality as yet one more example of oppression.

Feminists have distorted and ridiculed biblical standards such as submission and marriage and labeled them abhorrent.

Feminism has lied to us, telling us what's right and branding anyone who says otherwise as a closed-minded, right-wing bigot. We can become fearful of speaking up as a result. We are reminded of the story "The Emperor's New Clothes" by Hans Christian Andersen. In this classic tale, bogus weavers wove invisible clothing for the king to wear in an upcoming parade. The deceptive weavers bragged about their wares and said that only those too stupid or too unfit for employment would speak out negatively about their clothes. Not wanting to be thought of as stupid or unfit, the people went along with the lie. And the story goes on:

> No one wanted to let it appear that he could see nothing, for that would prove him not fit for his post. . . . So [the emperor] held himself more stiffly than ever, and the chamberlains held up the train that was not there at all.[9]

But even in the non-Christian world, women are finding the courage to speak up and say that they don't agree. Elizabeth Fox-Genovese, founder of the Institute for Women's Studies at Emory University, wrote a best-selling book called *Feminism Is Not the Story of My Life*,[10] about how today's feminist elite has lost touch with the real concerns of women. And because almost everything the feminist agenda endorses opposes biblical standards, we need to hold firmly to the truth. We need to be ready to scream from the rooftops, "Feminism *definitely* is not my life!"

But even when we do speak up, we're left wondering,

✻ What is my life?

✻ How do I respond to issues the feminists address?

✻ What are the biblical truths that counteract these cultural lies?

✻ What is the difference between being submissive and being trampled on?

✻ Do I really have to do as culture says and step on men to get ahead in my field?

✻ Should I demand equal rights at any cost?

✻ If I don't toot my own horn, who will?

It's pretty clear that feminism hasn't worked, but we need to find something that does. Something that answers questions like the ones above. Something that reconciles our need to be feminine with our right to fair treatment and the good points made by the feminist agenda. Something that helps us reclaim our true femininity as it was intended.

> **LYNDA** ✻ I was still in school when Betty Friedan made her mark on history, but my whole adult life has been impacted by its results. My generation botched the choices given to us through the feminist movement, and Rebecca's generation is destined to repeat these mistakes if we don't make some changes. ✻

One person at a time, we can either perpetuate the lie or we can change the course that feminism has set and reverse the damage for future generations.

Femininity As It Was Meant to Be

Friedan, like Smalley and Trent decades later, said women were too soft and needed to harden, too tender and needed to toughen. The problem was, the feminist movement swung women too far the other direction, and we encountered a new kind of imbalance.

The key to discovering our femininity as God planned it to be is in reclaiming the balance between toughness and tenderness. In chapter 2, we talked about the need to remain protected, and in chapter 3 the need to be intimate. True femininity embraces both these qualities in a fairly equal way. We need to be *tough,* in that we must be able to protect ourselves as well as our goals and dreams. We also need to be *tender* enough to find intimacy with God and others.

> **REBECCA** ❋ Years ago, I was devastated when a friend repeatedly lied to me and made me doubt everything else he had ever said. I let myself trust him but ended up feeling betrayed. One evening, I sat on my parents' bed crying to my mum. I recall saying that I didn't want to become hard, bitter, and shut off to this person. But as I said to her that night, "It hurts so bad to stay soft." ❋

Pain threatens our femininity, because the feminine woman has a side that is tender, open, and wisely trusting. In any painful situation, we have one of two choices: We can become overly tough and shut off to the point that we don't feel our pain and we allow bitterness to breed. Or we can stay open, grieve our hurt, and in so doing, keep our tender side tender.

> **LYNDA** ❋ I pinned down the tough side of my love as a single mom, but the tender side remained elusive. I still have to work every day on showing my tender side. Many other women I know are so gentle and compassionate that they get stepped on—a lot. Without the necessary boundaries of self-respect, their soft and gentle spirit opens them up to be taken advantage of by employers, friends, husbands, or children. We all need balance. ❋

The Bible describes the perfect love in God the Father as including both tough and tender dimensions of love. Take a look at Isaiah 40. Verse 10 tells us, "The Sovereign Lord comes with power, and his arm rules for him." But in the very next verse we read, "He tends his flock like a shepherd: He gathers the lambs in his arms and carries them close to his heart; he gently leads those that have young."[11]

We see that same connection between toughness and tenderness in the New Testament. In chapter 5 we'll discuss the inward—as well as outward—beauty described in 1 Peter 3:3-4: "Don't be concerned about the outward beauty that depends on fancy hairstyles, expensive jewelry, or beautiful clothes. You should be known for the beauty that comes from within." Verse 4 goes on to describe the unfading beauty of the truly feminine woman who possesses "a gentle and quiet spirit, which is so precious to God."

> **REBECCA** ✳ After doing a Greek study on what it means to be a 1 Peter 3:3-4 kind of woman, I discovered that SHE demonstrates a gentle and quiet spirit. That gentleness, which means meekness and humility, comes from being protected. SHE also exhibits a quiet spirit that stems from being at peace inside. The word *quiet* in Greek actually means "peaceable." SHE has a quiet confidence that is truly feminine. ✳

God wants us to be gentle and quiet—but spirited—women. God wants us to have a gentle strength. He wants us to demonstrate balance.

Deborah: Here Comes the Judge *(Judges 4–5)*

Long before women gained the right to vote or hold office, Deborah worked in a man's world. But her life reflected balance. Not only was she a wife, she also worked outside the home as a judge. As both a legal and spiritual counselor to the people whom God appointed her to serve, she judged in their disputes and led them in times of war. She was the only woman of the twelve judges who ruled during that era of Israel's history. Deborah had every opportunity to stand up for herself as an independent female and demand her equal rights, and in the process she could have grown tough and judgmental while neglecting her tender side. However, she chose a different response.

> God wants us to be gentle and quiet—but spirited—women.

Israel had seen better days; it was a bleak time in their history. For twenty years Jabin, king of Canaan, had ruthlessly oppressed the Israelites. His warriors had decimated the men, dishonored the women, and destroyed the children. Young people knew about freedom only from their parents, and for older people freedom was becoming just a distant memory. Downhearted and depressed, many of the Israelites turned to idols. They had slowly distanced themselves from God since their stronger days when they'd felt they didn't need Him. But now Jabin and his right-hand man, General Sisera, who commanded an army with nine hundred iron chariots, were breathing down their neck. Fearful and desperate, the Israelites grew more receptive to once again seeking God's help. That frame of mind made them open to Deborah's godly message in her role as mediator between God and His people.

Deborah's work as a judge took place in the hill country between Bethel and Ramah, a mountainous area where Sisera's chariots couldn't attack. Under a palm tree—later named after her—Deborah held court, judging the people and helping to guide them. Her competence in her work, however, came from her confidence in God and the balance she found in the midst of the many competing factors in her life.

And the result? God blessed the Israelites. They defeated Sisera and won their freedom. The occupation ended. The oppression ceased. Israel stayed free for the next forty years under Deborah's reign.

Femininity and You

Like Deborah, we live in a society that stands counter to our faith. Even more than today, Deborah's world belonged to men, so she likely heard the competing voices both within herself and from outside influences that said, "Get all you can get" and "You go, Girl, no matter what it takes to get there."

But God occupied first place in her life, a reality that daily helped her find balance. Her toughness allowed her as a woman to stay protected and hold her own in a man's world. Her tenderness kept her from trying to be a lone ranger. She invited others to have important roles too. We can learn from her example as a gentle, quiet—but spirited—woman by grasping some key truths.

1. When God creates me for an assignment, He also makes a way for me to become successful.

Lie: I have to be loud and aggressive in order to get anywhere in this world.

Deborah didn't need to step on men to get where she was. She merely lived up to her responsibilities, which had been given to her by God. Because her confidence was not based on natural strengths, natural things like wars and other people did not intimidate her, nor did the men who surrounded her. She voluntarily gave up her right to be in charge and acknowledged that the only rights she really had were the ones God gave her.

God promises that when you're faithful in the little things, He'll give you bigger responsibilities and opportunities.[12] You don't have to make your own way or knock people over to get there, and you don't have to get stressed out when you run into obstacles. They're God's battles, not yours.[13]

What passions ignite you and get your blood flowing? Talk to God about them and do what you can today to live out those passions wherever you are. Periodically check to see that you're tough enough not to let someone talk you out of these passions but tender enough not to knock others down while achieving them.

2. God-confidence is what I need to seek, and a balanced self-confidence will grow out of it.

Lie: I'm not confident and I never will be.

God-confidence marked Deborah's life. She knew God would give her the ability to perform the tasks He asked her to do.

REBECCA ✳ When I began in music, my dad, who is my manager, encouraged me in my concerts to share a few words before one of my songs. He stressed the importance of connecting in this way with the audience. On my first tour, at the age of thirteen, I memorized every line of my "speech." I'm sure it sounded to the audience as rehearsed as it was! At the time, I objected to having to do something that didn't come naturally. I could sing all day long on stage, but I had no confidence in my ability to speak before a crowd. But as I prayed to be used by God and practiced what I knew to be something I was called to do, despite my lack of self-confidence, my sharing grew to be natural and powerful. Today some people tell me that my words from the stage have had more impact on them than my music. *

If God has given you a job to do—whether it's in your home, at work, or at church—be confident and take the first steps toward achieving it. With Him, you have what it takes!

3. Wise and godly submission brings out the best in me.

Lie: If I'm submissive, I'll get trampled on.

Deborah must have understood the delicate balance between leading and submitting. Though she worked with others as a team, she did what God had called her to do at home and on the job. When it came time to fight, she gave the order: "Get ready!" she said to Barak. "Today the Lord will give you victory over Sisera, for the Lord is marching ahead of you."[14] At the same time, Deborah brought out the best in others. She freed Barak from having to compete and instead allowed him to excel at his own work. He accepted the challenge, but not without Deborah. His work ultimately got his name in among the heroes of the faith in Hebrews 11.[15]

God has called all of us to be submissive: "All of you be submissive to one another, and be clothed with humility, for God resists the proud, but gives grace to the humble."[16]

REBECCA * Though I know there is a God-honoring place for submission in my life, like you I still struggle at times in this area. Once while on my Romanian mission trip, I had been asked to carry a brand-new window from the car into the girls' home where I was working. One of the girls who lived there, a former street kid, had broken the window, and this was the replacement. Catalin, the man in charge of the home, asked me to put it on the floor in the stairwell landing. This didn't make sense to my practical woman mind. The floor was tiled. If the window fell over, it would be history. And kids were constantly flying down the stairwell, so there was a good chance it would get broken. I pointed this out to Catalin and asked if he'd prefer that I put it in a carpeted room instead. He said no, that it would be fine in the stairwell. I kept my mouth shut and then turned and carried the window . . . into the carpeted room! When Catalin found out what I had done, he made a tongue-in-cheek comment that marriage (and submission) might one day be a bit of an adjustment for me.

Though Catalin's comment was a friendly jab, the truth of it stuck with me. I should've recognized that it was his window and his home, and I should have respected his authority to have the last word—even when I thought my way was best. ✳

Submission means that we voluntarily acknowledge the leadership responsibilities of others. It doesn't mean we subordinate or take a permanent inferior position to someone else, whether that person is a boss, a husband, or a parent. Instead, we step aside and allow God to work through the gifts He's given them. It's their job not to exploit that trust or submission.[17]

If you have a boss, a husband, or a parent who abuses this submissive principle and lords over you, your tough side needs to kick in. Refuse to put yourself in physical or emotional danger. Never do something that betrays the things you believe in. If necessary, get help to know when to draw and enforce the line when the other person steps over it.

Ideally, in a God-led marriage, both husband and wife understand that decisions are a team effort. If a decision has been prayerfully considered by both spouses and their opinions remain different, the husband as the leader of the family has the final say, and that will require strengthening your tender side. Someone has to have the leadership role or chaos would result. So God gave that responsibility to the husband. If you're having trouble submitting to someone, pray that God will forgive you for your resistance, then ask for His guidance in making changes. Do it just because the Bible tells us to. *While* you do, God will work on the other person, and *when* you do, God will honor you for your obedience.

4. God made man and woman to complement each other.

Lie: As a woman, I will always have to compete with men.

Since the beginning of time, God's plan was for a woman and a man to work together. Woman was created to be a partner with man—equal to him, yet different. Suitable for him, capable of completing him. Complementing him, not competing with him.

> **REBECCA** ✻ From time to time, I visit a bed-and-breakfast for some rest and relaxation from my touring schedule. On a recent visit, I noticed a plaque on the wall of my room that beautifully depicts God's design for the man-woman relationship:
>
> > *The woman was made of a rib out of the side
> >   of Adam,*
> > *Not made out of his head to rule over him,*
> > *Nor out of his feet to be trampled upon by him,*
> > *But out of his side to be equal with him,*
> > *Under his arm to be protected,*
> > *And near his heart to be beloved.*
> > **Matthew Henry** ✻

Deborah worked with men as a unit, as part of God's team, with no part more important than another. Together they carried out God's orders and completed each other. Each gave in voluntarily to the other for the well-being of the entire nation. Together, Barak and Deborah climbed up the side of Mount Tabor and looked down to their enemies camped at the foot of the mountains.

Whether it's your marriage or your job, remember that you are working together on a team.[18] Even when the other player doesn't think this way, you can keep competition, envy, and bitterness in check by your actions. Remember, you can't change the other person, but you can change yourself by making sure both your tough and tender reactions remain intact. And the change in you might just help the other person eventually change too.

5. When I blame others, Satan—the real enemy—gets off scot-free.

Lie: Other people are to blame for my problems.

LYNDA ✳ I once lived near a couple who went through a hard time in their marriage. I'd get a call from either one at all times of the day or night telling me what the other had done wrong. Despite the fact that they were engaged in some pretty intense Christian marital counseling, their conflict continued. One night the wife appeared at my front door with more complaints about her husband's latest attacks. I picked up the phone and asked the husband to come, too. When he arrived, I seated them side by side on a couch, and then I plopped on a chair in front of them and said, "Satan is out to destroy your marriage. But while you two are going tit for tat with each other, he's getting away scot-free, and your boys are left suffering with the results." ✳

Deborah wisely recognized the enemy for who he was. She reminded the people that the fight was between the enemy and God, not the enemy and them.[19] This mentality kept their eyes on the common enemy and their all-powerful God, and away from each other. This focus kept them from becoming discouraged or from fighting the wrong battles.

To recognize the lies of Satan through the feminist agenda, you need to know the truth. Talk with godly older women. Look up and memorize Bible verses on topics that confuse you. Then you'll realize God's instruction on subjects such as abortion, homosexuality, gentleness, and submission.

As long as you look to yourself or others to be your strength, you will fail. As long as you look to others as the enemies, you will be distracted and taken away from your ultimate victory. Don't consider the foe to be your husband or your boss or even culture and the feminist agenda. See the enemy as Satan, then get busy defeating him at his own game. God's power in a Christian's life is greater than Satan's.[20]

✳

After the job was over and the battle was won, Deborah sang a song:

*When Israel's leaders take charge, and the people gladly
follow—bless the Lord! Lord, may all your enemies die as Sisera
did! But may those who love you rise like the sun at full strength![21]*

LYNDA ✳ I know a woman I'll call Angie who submitted to her un-
saved husband for twenty years by honoring and respecting his leadership role in their home. When her husband bullied her or made
unreasonable demands, five-foot-tall Angie got tough and drew necessary boundaries. But even when she stood her ground, she did it in a
tender, respectful way. She remained spirited—but she never lost her
gentleness and quietness either. At times her decisions didn't appear
to be making any difference and even seemed contrary to what she
should be doing. But as Angie worked on building the tough side of her
love, God protected her and worked on the tender side in her husband.
In year twenty-one of their marriage, Angie's husband, without a word,
was changed by the conduct of his godly, submissive wife. He's now a
lover of Jesus and a soul mate for Angie. ✳

The issue is not the feminist agenda as much as it is true femininity and balancing the tough and tender parts of your love. Allow
God to tenderize you enough to give and receive intimacy but toughen
you enough to achieve goals and protect others.

As you do, you'll find yourself becoming like Deborah—"the
sun at full strength!"[22] You'll find yourself becoming the gentle and
quiet—but spirited—woman God wants us SHEs to be.

✳ **SHEism** ✳ A truly feminine SHE is a woman
who balances her tough and tender sides of love, and in the
process SHE becomes a gentle and quiet—but spirited—
woman of God.

Additional Resources:

Diane Passno, **Feminism: Mystique or Mistake?** (Wheaton, Ill.: Tyndale
House Publishers, Inc., 2000)

Cynthia Hicks and Robert Hicks, **The Feminine Journey: Understanding the
Biblical Stages of a Woman's Life** (Colorado Springs: NavPress, 1994)

Part Two
HEALTHY

"Authentic beauty . . . is not ever to be discovered in the pomp and polish of high society, nor in the silk and satin of those conformed to popular culture. Rather, it emerges . . . in the life of a woman who is deeply in love with the Prince of her soul."

Leslie Ludy *Authentic Beauty*[1]

"Don't be concerned about the outward beauty that depends on fancy hairstyles, expensive jewelry, or beautiful clothes. You should be known for the beauty that comes from within."

1 Peter 3:3-4

Chapter 5

Beautiful: More than Skin-Deep

LYNDA ✳ I knew my daughter Courtney possessed some special physical qualities when she reached just under six feet tall by age thirteen. Her striking facial features along with her height caused people to stop her several times each week and ask if she was a model.

As her mom, I thought and prayed about this possibility often. What should I do? How do I help her learn the right lessons about life and beauty? In what way should I help her guard the decisions she makes and at the same time keep her from wondering in twenty years if she should have explored her modeling potential?

When Courtney was seventeen, at the persistence of a modeling agency in our hometown, she and I took a mother-daughter trip to Orlando to attend a modeling convention. The small agency represented Courtney and a few other teens. We arrived on July 3 and prepared for the next day's group runway competition.

Having served in Christian ministry and helped people concentrate on things that mattered for eternity, I felt uncomfortable watching young girls flip their hair over their shoulders and lick their lips—just in case the right person was watching. I had trouble processing the fact that these kids there were trying to find their big break—a break that I knew could ultimately break them.

The next day, I hemmed and ironed the military uniform Courtney was to wear on the runway. I draped it across her arm and hugged her as she headed off to the makeup area.

And then, the presentation. Lights went down and then came back up. Courtney stood on the left side of the stage with her right side facing the audience, head bowed, fingertips touching her hat. As the music started, she walked across the stage, and when she reached the runway, she turned and walked—no, slinked—toward the audience, and I couldn't believe what I saw.

Someone had completely unbuttoned Courtney's blouse, catching it only at the waist and angling up in a V toward her neck. The performance continued, but I can't tell you what happened. The lights went down again, and the models left the stage as I left the auditorium fighting back tears.

After settling my emotions, I confronted the heads of the modeling agency about how they had exploited my girl even though they knew our standards. I also informed them we would be withdrawing from the competition.

Courtney and I headed to Sarasota early the next morning, where I spent the day as a guest on one of the radio stations that carried my show. By the time we returned to Orlando, several well-known modeling agents around the world had called, and we met with two representatives from one New York agency. Their response to the previous day's runway experience was simple: "If that [experience] was uncomfortable for you, it all will be. Giorgio Armani would love you, Courtney. But the first thing he would do is have you remove your clothes and don a see-through raincoat. And frankly, if you don't do it, one hundred other girls will, and we will still get our paycheck."

Courtney's modeling days ended that day, but my own questions about beauty and how I teach others had only just begun. She acknowledged to me her mistake in allowing the agents to expose her, but she added, "It felt okay when there was no one else in the room." Courtney also told me how she had thought before we arrived that the officials would want her so badly that they'd allow her to choose what she would and wouldn't do.

Courtney's honesty struck a deep chord in me. I asked myself if I was living part of my life through Courtney's. Had my own failure at modeling during my college years caused me to want her to accomplish things I hadn't? Was I asking her to fulfill some of my unfulfilled dreams?

It appears that modeling is totally out of Courtney's system, even to the point that it's something she doesn't enjoy. But is the beauty thing in balance too? Does she have the right idea of what true beauty is? Will she use her beauty in the right way in the days to come? ✳

Beauty Then and Now

One thing every generation of women has had in common is our tenacious pursuit of beauty. Each era has defined the perfect woman in its own way and then held her up as a goal for everyone to achieve. In her classic book *American Beauty*, author Lois W. Banner wrote about the social history of the American ideal of the beautiful woman spanning two centuries. She said that during the nineteenth century, "Beauty for women represented not morality, but power."[2] Later that century, novels focused on marriages between working women and rich men, and articles featured lives of actresses who had risen from impoverished beginnings.

The beginning of the 1900s saw chorus girls glorified—rising from humble backgrounds to marry rich men. More complex makeup, hairstyles, and fashionable clothes became available to the common person. The idea of *beauty* or *belle* developed among both working and wealthy women to point out style setters.

Then beauty contests emerged, and in 1921 the United States witnessed the first Atlantic City Miss America Pageant. The event made a national ritual out of a belief, which persists today, that the pursuit of beauty should to be a woman's primary goal. This pageant became the dream of girls and the elusive goal of the average woman. And our quest for beauty marched on.

We don't have to search far to realize that the subject of beauty continues to be one of the most popular themes of our day too.

REBECCA ✳ During a recent trip to a bookstore, I noticed a headline on the current *Self* magazine that read, "Be Your Prettiest Self: How Tos." Even though my main reason for looking was for research on this book, I couldn't help noticing that somewhat familiar tug in- side—the questions that strike without warning and always raise self- doubts: "Do I measure up? Is even my *prettiest* self pretty enough?" So I turned to the right page to discover this particular magazine's secret to my prettiest self.

Meanwhile, *More* magazine boasted that it knew the "Eleven Biggest Beauty Breakthroughs." *Working Mother* magazine's main cover copy line read: "Don't Wait for Others to Sing Your Praises— Strut Your Stuff!" I counted more than eighty fashion and health maga- zines, and that didn't include those targeted to teens. ✳

More than ever before, today's woman has access to tools and techniques for achieving and maintaining beauty—exercise, diet, makeup, even cosmetic surgery. But where's the payoff of inner peace and contentment we expected?

A common message in movies and music screams to young girls and women alike: "You need to look a certain way—skinny, pretty, and stylish—and if you don't, you'd better do something about it." The results? Envy, competition, compromise, and low self-esteem.

LYNDA ✳ That's why I joined with thousands of other women chortling at an e-mail I read, which got revenge on the perfect Barbie image none of us is able to measure up to: Bifocal Barbie, Hot-flash Barbie, Facial-hair Barbie, and Flabby-arms Barbie. ✳

But what about you? Barbie is the least of our worries. Beauty images scream at us in every imaginable form. How do the impossi- ble-to-achieve plastic images you face every day affect the way you feel about yourself? How do you react to cultural or peer pressure? If as a mother you're obsessed about how you look, what message are you sending your daughter? And what about the dating scene? For teens and adults alike, the guys we date and marry are similarly bombarded by these unrealistic images and expectations. They subtly tell us that nothing less than that kind of beauty will do, and so the privileges and opportunities we've achieved as women continue to be overcast by a cloud of beauty failure. Best-selling author and researcher Naomi Wolf comments in her book, *The Beauty Myth:*

> *Recent research consistently shows that inside the majority of the West's controlled, attractive, successful working women, there is a secret "underlife" poisoning our freedom; infused with notions of beauty; it is a dark vein of self-hatred; physical obsessions; terror of aging and dread of lost control.*[3]

This fruitless search for perfection can be dangerous, and even fatal, as it manifests itself in women's lives today. For example, eating disorders exist at an all-time high. Women of all ages and stations in life struggle with anorexia and bulimia.

Maybe you haven't struggled with your body image to the point of developing an eating disorder. But do you ever feel envious of women who look better than you do, especially when they're strong where you're particularly weak? *She has muscular legs; I have skinny ones. She has blue eyes; mine are mousy brown. She's tall and willowy; I'm short and squatty.*

To compensate for these perceived weaknesses, many women respond with immodest dress, flirtatious behavior, promiscuity, sexual addictions, and other destructive actions—and these outward displays of inward failures are not limited to teens.

LYNDA ✳ As I get older, I'm adding aging to the beauty battles I'm already fighting. I'm well aware of my own struggles; whether yours include weight gain, wrinkles, or gray hair . . . the list can seem endless to all of us. It's easy to fall into the trap of spending too much time, money, and effort trying to beautify ourselves, when what we discover is that we're out of time and money, and the feelings of failure and discontent remain. Nothing really satisfies. ❋

Let's Face It . . . Beauty *Does* Matter to Us

Truth time: If you're like most breathing women, when you're in public you often subtly (or not so subtly!) check out the people in your surroundings to see if any of them are checking you out.

We're not here to tell you that beauty doesn't matter, but to assure you that it's okay to seek beauty within balance. From the beautiful Garden God created for us to the mansions we'll one day live in and the streets of gold we'll walk upon with our Savior, we're designed for beauty.

But we've got to put beauty in its right perspective! This chapter is about freedom. Freedom from our culture's bondage and impossible standards. Freedom from past lies that told you your worth depended on how you look. Freedom from the bondage of wrong actions that spring from our desire to be beautiful. And freedom from the Christian mantra that sometimes says outward appearance doesn't matter—when it really does, in balance.

> **LYNDA** ❋ I know one woman, now in her fifties and nearly two hundred pounds overweight, whose preacher father caught her "primping" one day in front of a mirror when she was a teen, and he beat her with a belt. From that extreme to the overused message that we should concentrate *solely* on the inside, many of us have squelched the desire in us to be beautiful and now see it as a hopeless cause. An extreme example, but I can understand the effect her father's message may have had on her. ❋

Here are a couple of not-so-drastic examples you may be able to relate to. Two beautiful, successful, professional women in the forty to fifty age range. Two women with qualities their peers could envy.

Mary: When I was growing up, my self-esteem on any given day was greatly affected by how attractive I was feeling. Beauty is a very high value in nature, art, and music, as well as in people, especially women. Successful, happy women are beautiful on TV and in movies. So, to be accepted, approved, and attract opportunity and success, I thought I had to use every means possible to be outwardly beautiful.

Debra: When I was a gawky child, my father put me down verbally. And though I could see I was pretty on the outside, I didn't feel pretty throughout my growing-up years. Then as an adult in Houston, Texas, where beautiful ladies were everywhere, I watched women compete with each other to be the most beautiful, whether in the grocery store or at the health club. It didn't take long to realize that the prettiest received the most preferential treatment, and brains weren't necessary to become a trophy on a man's arm. But as I aged along with the beautiful others around me, I watched them go to all kinds of extremes to preserve the only thing they possessed—outward beauty.

In his best-selling book *Wild at Heart,* John Eldredge states:

Not every woman wants a battle to fight, but every woman yearns to be fought for. . . . She wants to be more than noticed, she wants to be wanted. She wants to be pursued. . . . Every woman wants to have a beauty to unveil. Not to conjure, but to unveil. Most women feel the pressure to be beautiful from very young, but that is not what I speak of. There is also a deep desire to simply and truly be the beauty, and be delighted in."[4]

Yes, every woman wants to be beautiful . . . to be romanced and rescued. When it doesn't happen, we learn to pretend. Pretend it doesn't matter. Pretend I feel okay about myself. Pretend I don't ache to be noticed and told I'm special and beautiful. That's when our unhealthy responses begin.

LYNDA ❋ After my first husband left, I pretended it didn't matter and I was still okay and attractive and desirable. But much of me wanted to stay behind and convince others that I had been a beautiful wife and daughter-in-law and mother. Nagging in the back of my mind, however, were voices that reminded me of every insecurity I'd ever felt.

Every corner I'd ever cowered in. Every word I'd left unsaid for fear of bringing attention to the parts of me that were my unbeautiful, undesirable, not-worth-keeping self. *What's wrong with me?* I wondered.

I surrendered my life to Christ within the month after my husband had left. That September in 1985, prayer changed my life, but not all at once. One day at a time—through prayer, Bible reading, and association with other vibrant Christian women—I concentrated on finding out who I was to Jesus. While I spent time on these issues, somehow it helped resolve other insecurities as well. God took care of defending me to others, and by sprucing up my inside beauty, my outside beauty improved too. When the nagging voices of insecurity speak to me even today, I have to keep running back to my Father for help in different areas. ✳

REBECCA ✳ I've also struggled with my self-image. Being involved in the entertainment business, where image counts way too much, has only made matters worse. I've never been fine-featured or petite. My mom has always said I have "heavy bones." As I grew older, I felt this more keenly whenever I'd perform. I felt all the TV-induced insecurities that almost every other modern girl feels. Compared to the glamorous women I saw in the media, I was too "shapely," too "healthy" looking. I truly believe that if it wasn't for God's protection and my family's accountability, I could've started down an extremely dangerous and excessive path of trying to lose weight. I've got to be reminded constantly of the difference between internal and external beauty. ✳

God spoke about these two kinds of beauty hundreds of years ago regarding the difference between how He looks at a person and the world's view: "The Lord doesn't make decisions the way you do! People judge by outward appearance, but the Lord looks at a person's thoughts and intentions."[5] Obviously the tendency to judge on outward appearance has been an ongoing issue, because the Bible addresses it again generations later in the New Testament:

Don't be concerned about the outward beauty that depends on fancy hairstyles, expensive jewelry, or beautiful clothes. You should be known for the beauty that comes from within.[6]

Before you groan and say you already know all this, hang in there with us and see why it's a topic worth talking about. Let's put it in writing so it's staring us in the face. What are some differences between external and internal beauty?

External Beauty	Internal Beauty
Can be destroyed by accident or age	Renewed day by day
Finite	Eternal
Deteriorates with time	Timeless
Intimidates others	Affirms others
Static	Growing

Holistic beauty is a package deal—a blend of both external and internal beauty. It's possible to have one without the other. And in this truth lies a secret to beauty that can change your life: Internal beauty amplifies external beauty. But that truth doesn't necessarily work in reverse; a physically attractive person may have a very ugly character.

As women, we're designed to want others to admire us and affirm our beauty—as well as to appreciate who we are. It's our natural instinct to focus on beautifying our external appearance, so most of us need to be more deliberate about submitting to God to allow Him to beautify us on the inside.

> Internal beauty amplifies external beauty.

Take this quiz to check out your beauty pulse internally, externally, and holistically:

Quick Beauty Quiz

Answer yes or no to each of the following questions:

1. Do you feel comfortable enough in your own skin to be around close family and friends without always having to wear makeup?

2. Do you often feel beautiful or pretty?

3. Can you eat a dessert without feeling any guilt?

4. Can you see an attractive girl or woman and not feel jealous or compare yourself to her?

5. Do you feel that you are doing a good job of balancing your focus on both inner and outer beauty?

6. Have you avoided laxative abuse and regularly skipping meals to lose weight?

7. Are you purge-free?

8. Can you view slim, seemingly flawless women on TV and in magazines without feeling an overwhelming sense of disappointment in yourself?

9. Would you say that for the most part you have a positive, healthy self-image?

10. Do you feel that you have a good understanding of holistic beauty?

Scoring: Count the number of "yes" responses that you made.

10 Wonderful! Your self-image and sense of holistic beauty in God is excellent.

7–9 You are doing quite well at keeping your beauty perspective balanced. This chapter will be a good reminder and challenge for you.

4–6 Your excessive outer-appearance focus is definitely crippling your inner growth and beauty. Give serious attention to this chapter and talk to a Christian mentor about how you can apply its truths.

0–3 Sister, we've gotta chat. You need healing in this area of your life. You're due for some heart-to-heart time with a godly older woman who can help you accept yourself for how God made you.

> **LYNDA** ✳ Two passages in the Bible are particularly challenging to me. They keep me ever stretching and never quite attaining. One is 1 Corinthians 13, which reminds me that my ability to love isn't what it should be until I can consistently do such things as be patient and kind

and not be jealous, proud, or score-keeping. The other passage is
Proverbs 31. On my worst days I want to have a private word with the
woman described there. "Thanks, Mrs. Superwoman, the rest of us
have been straining at your bar ever since." But on my best days, I'd
like to sip a latte with her and thank her for setting such high standards
for us as women. For reminding us that we *are* to be constantly stretch-
ing for the higher mark, to look more like Christ, and to become truly
beautiful SHEs. ✻

The bad news is that no woman has ever been born a SHE,
whether her issues involve perceived beauty failure, weakness, low
self-esteem, or misuse of beauty. But the good news is that God can
transform all of us into SHEs. Let's take a closer look at a real-life but
long-time-ago example of how God did just that.

Bathsheba: Beauty on a Rooftop (2 Samuel 11:1–12:25)

Bathsheba was a woman in the Old Testament who was born
with plenty of external beauty. She doesn't get a ton of play time in
the Bible, but what she did certainly has left its mark. She grew up in a
good home. Bathsheba's husband, Uriah, was an honored and cele-
brated hero in the king's army.

Then one spring day, Bathsheba's life changed forever. King David, who usually accompanied his army to battle, decided for some
reason to send them on while he remained behind in Jerusalem. One
afternoon after a nap, he got out of bed and walked to the palace roof,
where he saw her bathing on another nearby rooftop. David asked
around to find out who she was and then sent his messengers to sum-
mon Bathsheba for a palace visit. She went.

Do you wonder whether Bathsheba purposely placed herself
within David's view? Why would she bathe in view of others? Did she
use her looks to get the guy? We don't know whether she flaunted her
beauty; what we do know is that she didn't guard her heart or obey
God's standards out of an inner, godly beauty. God had chosen David
based on his internal character, not the externals. David was described as a man after God's own heart.[7]

A man with this kind of heritage from God made a huge mistake that day with Bathsheba. And she, with her wonderful heritage, was not innocent either. They slept together and she got pregnant. As so often happens, one bad choice led to another, and wanting to cover his tracks, David sent her husband to the front lines of battle. David gave the command. Uriah died. Bathsheba mourned. Then Bathsheba and David married, and their son was born. That's when the consequences hit.

Scripture records that David's part in these wrongs was the worst sin he ever committed.[8] This big blemish took place in an otherwise godly life and through a woman who misused her beauty. Their sin started a chain reaction of sorrow and curses on their family, including the death of David and Bathsheba's son and later three of David's other sons.[9]

But somewhere along the line, Bathsheba repented. And somewhere along the line, God accepted her repentance, exchanged her sin for His grace, and then turned that sin into something He could use for His glory.

Here's the kicker. Check out Proverbs 31:10-31. How does Scripture describe this wonder-woman? She is virtuous, trustworthy, industrious, generous, strong, joyful, wise, kind, and God-fearing. As a result, her husband trusts her, she enriches his life, and she's "worth more than precious rubies."[10]

So who is this woman?

Scripture tells us that King Lemuel, inspired by his mother, wrote this chapter. Some Bible scholars have said that King Lemuel was Solomon. And Solomon's mother was none other than Bathsheba—the woman whose inner beauty needed to develop so it was strong enough to guide and enhance her outer beauty.

But the forgiven version of that woman is the one godly women still emulate today.

Bathsheba's story began with her outer beauty, which she used for destruction, and it ends with her inner beauty, which she used for good: "Charm is deceptive, and beauty does not last; but a woman who fears the Lord will be greatly praised."[11]

Between the Bath"she"ba and the Bath"SHE"ba came repentance. God honored her repentance and provided His grace. Then He went on to use the situation—and ultimately BathSHEba's beauty—for His glory. SHE appears among the ancestors of Jesus Christ, the Savior of the world.

Beauty and You

So what does Bathsheba's story have to do with you and me?

Like Bathsheba, all of us have been given a measure of beauty, and all of us have misused it at one time or another. Maybe you've become enslaved to some type of eating disorder. Maybe you've allowed yourself to become consumed with envy or low self-esteem. Perhaps you've given in to using immodest dress, flirtatious behavior, promiscuity, or even sexual addictions to feel attractive and beautiful.

It's much easier to get trapped by the negatives and by your failures instead of focusing on the freedom Christ gives you to enjoy being yourself. Today's the day to grab hold of God's truth and live it!

·· ✳ *SHE Lives the Truth* ✳ ··

1. God sees me as perfectly made.

Lie: I'm ugly. I'll never measure up to others.

Every woman has something she doesn't like about herself. Ask any model, and she'll list the things that bother her about her own body. There's good news about our flaws, but only Christians can fully realize and live out that good news. Second Corinthians 12:9-10 acknowledges our weak places and even says we can boast about them. Why? Because where we're weak, God can become strong. If everything were perfect in our life and body, we wouldn't need a Savior. History has shown that when things are good, we as humans go our own way and do our own thing. That's why the fact that life ain't perfect and neither are we is good news. Your imperfections on the outside can be some of the very things God uses to polish you up on the inside.

That isn't, however, carte blanche to neglect the outside. We do have a responsibility to take care of our body and to make the most of what we've been given. After all, we're the Holy Spirit's temple.[12] With an appropriate amount of dieting and exercise, and trips to the mall, gym, hair salon, and makeup counter, anyone can improve her appearance. But overdoing the beautification of our outward appearance means we underdo improvements in other areas of our life.

Picture your body as a well-tended garden. You're the gardener, working to bring pleasure to the Master who owns the garden. Now think: What if you were to constantly water your flower bed? The flowers would drown. What if you constantly covered them with fertilizer? They'd suffer chemical burn. What if you constantly stood over your garden, fussing and fretting, pulling at the flowers and leaves? You'd block the sun. All this over-gardening would do is stunt the garden's growth. In the same way, overfussing about your appearance blocks the Son from growing you, too.

If you feel your arms are too skinny or your thighs are too fat, concentrate instead on the beautiful eyes or hair you have. When you come across a mirror at home or out in public, make a habit of not glancing at yourself in the reflection. Discouragement inevitably hits when you focus on perceived flaws. Regularly surrender your flaws or weaknesses to God, then concentrate instead on the good things God has blessed you with and the opportunities He's placed in your path for that moment.[13]

Because of what God has given you, your beauty is perfect! That includes what you see as imperfections. Pray that God will help you see yourself the way He sees you, accept yourself the way He accepts you, and live out your beauty as He designed you to live.

2. My outer beauty can be gone in a moment. Inner beauty never goes away.

Lie: When I look good, I have just about everything.

"Don't store up treasures here on earth, where they can be eaten by moths and get rusty, and where thieves break in and steal. Store your treasures in heaven, where they will never become moth-eaten or rusty and where they will be safe from thieves. Wherever your treasure is, there your heart and thoughts will also be."[14] While these verses are generally associated with physical possessions, they

> Outer beauty can be gone in a moment. Inner beauty never goes away.

can certainly apply to beauty, too. Not only will every woman's outward attractiveness fade as she grows older, but there's always the possibility of an accident, illness, or injury to destroy her outward beauty while she is young.

REBECCA ❋ I had a scare along these lines a few years ago. During a particularly strenuous time of touring, I fell ill with Bell's palsy, thought to be a virus that attacks facial nerves coming from the brain. Doctors still aren't sure what causes it, but it's often attributed to extreme stress. Whatever the source, I awoke one morning to find myself unable to control one side of my lips, unable to raise my right eyebrow, and unable to drink from a cup without spilling. My looks, which I'd taken for granted and are important to the work I do, were in jeopardy.

I did regain complete control of my facial muscles, but some, like Joni Eareckson Tada, never get a second chance at undamaged outward beauty. In the years since her diving accident that caused her paralysis, Joni learned a lesson that most of us are still working on: that lasting beauty comes from the inside out. And no one is more beautiful than Joni. I'll never again see the way I look on the outside the same way. Any assets I possess could be gone in an instant, so more than ever I must invest in "makeup" for the inside. That means crawling up into Jesus' lap and talking with Him regularly, reading His word, and spending time with others who have also gone to Him for a master makeover. ❋

Even if an accident, illness, or injury doesn't harm your outer beauty, age will in time.

LYNDA ❋ When I read "Though our bodies are dying, our spirits are being renewed every day,"[15] I'm certain the apostle Paul must have been addressing a room full of menopausal women when he wrote these words! He might just as well have said, "The bad news is you've got a few more wrinkles and gray hair. The good news is . . ." ❋

Since even the rich can't fight age, it's time to get smart. Invest in the brand of beauty that you can always afford and will never get old or sag or wrinkle or fade. Galatians 5:22-23 provides the secret to the inner fountain of youth: "When the Holy Spirit controls our lives, he will produce this kind of fruit in us: love, joy, peace, patience, kindness, goodness, faithfulness, gentleness, and self-control."

Start a new project for yourself over the next nine months. Take one gift of the Spirit each month. Look up each word in your Bible concordance and find verses that describe more about it. Memorize at least one of these verses. Pray that God would grow this fruit in your life. Then watch for places to plug it in. Keep a journal and write down ways you find God working in this area. When you do this, you will have discovered the nine secrets to eternal internal beauty that will never fade.

3. Despite the ways I may have abused my body or misused my beauty, God loves and forgives me and makes me new.

Lie: I've messed up my life. I can never be beautiful on the inside again.

REBECCA ✳ Based on what I perceived as personal body flaws in myself, I realized that no girl is beyond abusing her body through excessive dieting, laxative abuse, or binging and purging. It just takes pushing the right buttons. My mom is most encouraging and affirming in this area. She listens to me share my insecurities and encourages me to be balanced in my eating, not to skip meals, and to exercise when I can. Just knowing that she's watching keeps me accountable. ✳

Bathsheba probably would have found Proverbs 31:30 to be true as she grew older: "Charm is deceptive, and beauty does not last; but a woman who fears the Lord will be greatly praised." When she repented, she experienced God's grace and acceptance. The process of healing from your misuse is the same as it was for Bathsheba.

MISUSE
Recognize the ways you've abused your focus on appearance.

REPENTANCE
Ask God to forgive you.

GRACE
Realize that God not only loves to forgive but also to make things new. His grace cleans our slate.

ACCEPTANCE
Start over, seeing yourself through God's eyes from this point forward. Know your place before God and in God.

❋

REBECCA ❋ I once read this particularly powerful article in an Australian devotional:

> Simple Truths Are So Good
>
> A beauty product company once asked people in a large city to send pictures, along with brief letters, describing the most beautiful women they knew. Within weeks, thousands of letters came in.
>
> One letter caught the attention of the employees and was soon passed on to the company president. It was written by a boy from a broken home, who lived in a rundown neighborhood. With lots of spelling corrections, an excerpt from his letter read: "A beautiful woman lives down the street from me. I visit her every day. She makes me feel like the most important kid in the world. We play checkers and she listens to my problems. She understands me. When I leave she always yells out the door that she's proud of me." The boy ended his letter by saying, "This picture shows you that she is the most beautiful woman in the world, and one day I hope I have a wife as pretty as her."
>
> Intrigued by the letter, the president asked to see the woman's picture. His secretary handed him the photograph of a smiling, toothless woman, well advanced in years, sitting in a wheelchair. Sparse gray hair was pulled back in a bun. The wrinkles that formed deep furrows on her face were somehow diminished by the twinkle in her eyes.
>
> "We can't use this woman!" exclaimed this president,

smiling. "She would show the world that our products aren't necessary to be beautiful."[6] ❊

This woman had found the secret to internal beauty. At the end of the day, that's what we all hope to find. Beauty is truly more than skin-deep. It's down inside where God looks on the heart. And when He gets access to the inside, the outside changes too. What a deal— two for the price of one.

Rise up, my beloved, my fair one, and come away. For the winter is past, and the rain is over and gone. The flowers are springing up, and the time of singing birds has come, even the cooing of turtledoves. The fig trees are budding, and the grapevines are in blossom. How delicious they smell! Yes, spring is here! Arise, my beloved, my fair one, and come away.

My dove is hiding behind some rocks, behind an outcrop on the cliff. Let me see you; let me hear your voice. For your voice is pleasant, and you are lovely.

Song of Songs 2:10-14

❊ **SHEism** ❊ A truly beautiful SHE is a woman who honors God with her holistic—inward and outward— beauty.

"There is a dullness, monotony, sheer boredom in all of life when virginity and purity are no longer protected and prized. By trying to grab fulfillment everywhere, we find it nowhere."

Elisabeth Elliot *Passion and Purity*[1]

"God has called us to be holy, not to live impure lives. Anyone who refuses to live by these rules is not disobeying human rules but is rejecting God, who gives his Holy Spirit to you."

1 Thessalonians 4:7-8

Pure: Thwarting Temptation

LYNDA ✳ Amanda from California called in to my radio program to make a comment about our topic regarding the lies women believe. Amanda talked about wanting to find God's will regarding finances for relocating and whether or not she should marry her fiancé. She asked that I call her to chat personally by phone.

I did get back with Amanda, and she repeated the needs she wanted me to pray with her about. As we talked, more of her circumstances came to light. She'd been living with her fiancé for five years, and they had two children together. Amanda wanted God to bless her while she remained in sexual sin.

I talked to Amanda about her need to make some changes before she could expect God's blessings. I compared a godly life to baking a loaf of banana bread: "You don't include green beans and peanuts in the recipe," I said. "If you do, you'll never get banana bread." The same is true of a holy life in that she must include only the holy ingredients. This excludes sexual sin and all other sins of the body and mind.

"Does all this make sense to you?" I asked Amanda.

"Yes," she said, "but it's too hard. I need [my fiancé] too much." ✳

Culture bombards all of us daily with immoral solutions to life's problems, and we often let the lies convince us to compromise and comply with their standards—or lack of them. How are you doing in the area of purity?

✳ Do you have trouble believing that God has your best interest at heart with the sexual rules He established, or do you feel He's trying to keep you from sexual enjoyment?

✳ Do you believe sexual purity is a myth and impossible for you to obtain?

✳ Do you struggle with lust?

✳ Do you masturbate?

✳ Seeking to feel more attractive, do you dress immodestly?

✳ Do you struggle with impure thoughts regularly?

✳ Do you often expose your mind to different kinds of impure images?

✳ Are you toying with the idea of an adulterous affair, or are you single and involved sexually with someone?

LYNDA ✳ Amanda's situation continued to weigh on my heart long after our phone conversation ended. Anger overwhelmed me at the thought of the familiar cycle of sin ravaging yet another person's life. ✳

Scripture tells us that "evil desires lead to evil actions, and evil actions lead to death."[2]

First evil desires then evil actions then death.

If sin is still fun it's not finished yet. The forever end result of sin is death.

Sexual sin isn't the only outgrowth of lust—or evil desires. Impurity and compromise show their ugly face in all kinds of forms and cause sin we might not label as such. Alcoholism destroys bodies and marriages and lives. Drug abuse ravages young and old alike. Food addictions damage health and often kill. Slander, foul language, lies, and dirty talk also cripple and ultimately destroy people and relationships.

> If sin is still fun it's not finished yet.

All these start with simple lusts or temptations or evil desires that seem harmless on the surface. But when we act on them instead of turning and running, they eventually bring death. Death of a marriage. Death of a relationship. Death of a conscience.

The Bible lists countless examples of sin's effects. Eve looked at the fruit, and then she looked back and saw it was "good for food and pleasing to the eye."[3] Sin and ultimate death resulted.[4] Similarly, Samson "saw a woman,"[5] then he looked at her again and asked his father and mother to "get her for me, for she looks good to me."[6] Later on he fell in love with Delilah, which ultimately cost Samson his life.[7] Lust conceived, gave birth to sin, and then led to death.

Sexual sin is perhaps the most damaging and most pervasive form of impurity. It's also the one we want to focus on in this chapter. Because sexual sin affects us in unique ways beyond the effects of other types of sin, Satan works overtime in this particular area of our life.[8]

Purity Defined—and Undefined

Sex screams at us from every part of our culture. Movies, TV, billboards, magazines, and modems use sex to sell everything from Pepsi to politics.

REBECCA ✳ Recently I experienced this unfortunate phenomenon after flipping through my brother's hunting magazine. An attractive blonde woman was featured in a sexy pose on the back cover ad for a bow and arrow! ✳

Of the thousands of references, innuendos, and jokes the average person sees on movies and TV, few if any deal with either married sex or problems resulting from casual physical involvement. Our society has made sex a mandatory component of happiness and fulfillment, but what we discover instead is that it satisfies only for a short time, while its consequences, when indulged in outside of marriage, live on.

Since time began, people have tried to find ways to keep sinning without having to deal with—or even acknowledge—the potential consequences. The myth of "safe sex" has turned up everywhere with its lying message. From the classroom to the boardroom, people are buying into the misconception that a condom will protect against sin's results. But the only thing safe sex has done is add confusion, failure, and fuel to keep the cycle going. Noted speaker and abstinence advocate Tony Campolo wrote, "With Sex Ed, we show you how to do it, then we warn you not to do it—but we tell you if you decide to do it, to be careful, because it could kill you, make you sick, produce an unwanted baby. Talk about confusion!"[9]

> **REBECCA** ❊ I have a huge passion for the issue of sexual purity. So much so that I've spoken about it at almost all of my concerts for the past ten years. It's an issue that spans all marital, economic, and age differences. I've written a song about it and a book called *Wait for Me.*[10] My passion for this issue is fueled by seeing so many in my generation being ripped off by Satan. He has promoted his lies far too well, and too few believers are talking about and living the truth that combats those lies. I've spoken to college students in Kyrgyzstan, to a downtown club audience in Paris, and to thousands of people elsewhere around the world about the fact that I'm a virgin and am waiting until marriage for sex. Yet I could count on one hand the number of times I've caught any flak for speaking up on this issue. I believe that deep down, most people respect those who stand for purity, and underneath it all, they know it's the right way to go. ❊

Wholeness and health accompany purity. It's the only way to break sin's cycle of devastation and death. Unadulterated, undiluted, unspoiled—all are synonyms for *pure*. Webster's dictionary defines *pure* as: unmixed with any other matter; free from what weakens or pollutes; containing nothing that does not properly belong; free from moral fault or guilt.[11]

The definition is clear on paper, but in real life it gets much more fuzzy and gray. We spoke with Leslie Yeaton, international abstinence trainer for Focus on the Family. Leslie became pregnant at sixteen, experienced two failed marriages, and is now mother to two adult children and grandmother of three. Leslie travels the world teaching a message of passionate purity. Leslie says that the problem with defining purity is that it must be *redefined* today. Leslie alluded to President Clinton's 1997 statement, which inferred that it's okay to engage in sexual activity as long as intercourse is not involved. More recently, secretary of state Colin Powell spoke to the youth of the world in an MTV audience saying, "Let's just be real here. . . . You can't abstain from sex." Former U.S. surgeon general Joycelyn Elders said, "We've taught our children what to do in the front seat of a car, now we need to teach them what to do in the backseat."

Even the True Love Waits pledge has been forced to alter and further clarify its definition of purity. According to officials at the True Love Waits headquarters, the pledge was revised because the abstinence movement had noted growing misconceptions by youth and adults about what is meant by "abstain from sex." They acknowledged the huge increase in people involved in oral sex and other acts of intimacy who believed they were still virgins because they hadn't actually had intercourse. The new pledge includes abstinence from intercourse as only part of the purity definition.

Author Ed Young writes about the new and unimproved definition of purity: "While pure once described a person of almost saintly character, it is now most often used to describe not people, but things. 'That is so pure,' a young person might say today with a hint of admiration, even awe. What does it mean? If something is pure, what is it? At the very least, it's strong, undiluted, and inarguably fine. It's powerful and worthy of respect."[12]

The results of an online poll of *Seventeen* magazine readers appearing in the August 2003 issue echoed the fact that purity and sex in general have been redefined. Of those surveyed, 56 percent said they didn't think oral sex was sex. Thirty-one percent said they've been to parties where oral sex was the norm, and 9 percent said they've participated in it.[13] But what used to be sex is still sex, according to Dr. Peter Leone of the University of North Carolina at Chapel Hill. "It's sex," he declares. "It's sex because it's genital contact—that's it. If something involves how people feel about themselves sexually, and it involves sex organs, then it's sex."[14]

The Downward Spiral

Sexual temptation is nothing new, but its encroachment and effects have grown more serious.

> **LYNDA** ✳ When I was in my late teens, I watched a sitcom called *That Girl* starring Marlo Thomas. I liked watching Marlo's character, Ann Marie, and her boyfriend, Donald, date in a clean and wholesome way. I didn't question the way they did things. Network rules demanded that before each episode ended, Donald had to be seen leaving her apartment, and kisses—their only physical contact—could last just a couple of seconds.
>
> Now it seems that most TV shows highlight characters constantly jumping in and out of bed and sampling partners like a buffet. Even program titles such as *Sex in the City* encourage immorality. It all makes the predecessor to such attitudes—the free-love hippie movement from the sixties—pale by comparison. ✳

Sex is an especially sensitive issue because it involves our body as well as our soul, our spirituality—the deepest part of who we are. Sex also involves a relationship with someone else, and with each sexual encounter, a part of each partner forever remains stuck to the other. But culture doesn't want us to realize this truth. Richard Foster writes, "They totally eliminate relationship and restrain sexuality to the narrow confines of the genitals. They have made sex trivial."[15]

And women in their twenties, thirties, and forties are dealing with the aftermath of this promiscuity. Sexually transmitted diseases are at epidemic levels. STDs carried by pregnant women can infect their baby. Newborns infected with syphilis or herpes may suffer severe birth defects.

It makes sense, as Randy Alcorn wrote, "Purity is always smart; impurity is always stupid. Not sometimes. Not usually. Always. . . . There are no exceptions."[16]

Sin strips away the safe shelter of purity. In order to avoid the deathly consequences of sin, we must recognize its insidious assaults on our own life. We must recognize and then nip it in the bud. The assault begins with lust.

Impurity's Tools of the Trade

Lust, or mind sex, is mental promiscuity that depersonalizes sex and dehumanizes people. Masturbation is a form of mind adultery that draws many into its selfish web of lust. And pornography not only degrades women, but feeds unrealistic images to a man's mind that work only to destroy intimacy in marriage. A survey taken at a Promise Keepers gathering of 1,500 Christian men revealed that half of those polled admitted they had viewed pornography during the previous week.[17] Talk to men and women about the first time they accidentally came across pornography? Not only can they tell you their age, but they probably remember where they were and what they saw. Images fed to our mind are powerful and hard to erase. Chuck Swindoll defines lust as "an overpowering desire to enter into the actual fulfillment of one's fantasy."[18]

> Compromise multiplied equals life-injuring mistakes. Can we pinpoint the individual choices that lead to those mistakes?

Lust happens in increments. Baby steps, if you will. A little lust of this, a little lust of that. One small indulgence combined with one seemingly insignificant compromise. Giving in a little one time and a little more another. Before you know it, sin has taken over. And compromise multiplied equals life-injuring mistakes. It's easy for us to describe in detail the wrong moves we've made, but can we pinpoint the individual choices that led to them? If we can learn to see and resist the early compromises, we're on our way to preventing the mistakes. Our goal, then, is to become good compromise spotters, to stay on our toes and defend our purity at all costs.

Mary of Nazareth's Letter to You (Luke 1–2; 23–24)

Imagine if Mary of Nazareth were to write a letter to us:

Dear Sisters:

Hello, I'm Mary, and I wanted to talk to all of you reading this chapter on purity. You know me as the mother of Jesus, and many call me "the Virgin Mary." Though I lived in a different time, I know how we women stick together, and you need to know how my experience still affects what can happen to you today.

I wasn't born into financial wealth or social status, but my Jewish heritage made me rich. I learned God loved His people, and I learned He loved me. I grew to love Him too, and I wanted to please Him. So I lived by His standards, pure in every way I knew. When I made mistakes, I sought His forgiveness. I wanted to be ready for Him to use me. I didn't want to mess up His perfect plan for my life. And my, what a plan that was!

I was a virgin when the angel Gabriel told me I would give birth to the long-expected Messiah. Imagine my surprise when I realized the everlasting Son of the Father would be born through me![19]

As I look back on my life, I wonder what message I should give to you.

It's not Jesus' birth in a manger in Bethlehem,[20] though I would ponder the splendor of that event all of my life.[21]

It's not forty days later, when we took Him to the Temple to be dedicated as our firstborn—and when I met Simeon and the prophetess Anna, who warned me about the pain that lay ahead for me.[22]

It's not when Jesus was twelve and He disappeared in a Passover crowd, or the eighteen years that followed as Jesus continued to grow in wisdom and stature.[23] People no longer called Him the carpenter's son.

It's not the Crucifixion, where in His dying moments, I felt a sword piercing my soul as Simeon had foretold.

It's not even the days after the Resurrection, when I prayed with other faithful followers in the upper room in Jerusalem and saw the bigger picture of what Jesus' life would mean to all people.[24]

As wonderful as all these events were, and as privileged as I was to experience them, my message to you is more personal. The title "Virgin Mary" refers to my sexual purity, but dealing with temptations like you find today, I couldn't have stayed pure without purity of heart. And I couldn't keep a pure heart without:

Faith. Even before my encounter with Gabriel and discovering I would bear the Messiah, I chose to be faithful to God. I decided to trust that He knew and would do what was best for me and would not withhold anything good from me. Even when I didn't know the exact direction my life would take or how God's plan would unfold, even when things didn't appear to be going well, and even when I stood in front of my Son as He was dying on the cross, I chose to trust.

Humility. Humility doesn't come naturally to human beings—especially us women. I had to constantly remind myself of my commitment to God and that it wasn't about me. Being willing to serve God meant He needed a holy and pure follower, completely surrendered to His higher, holier will. That meant humility.

Reverence. The angel explained that God was pleased with my choices to obey Him. In those moments, I could have doubted God or questioned His methods and plan for my life. Instead, I determined more than ever to turn everything over to Him as my God. I revered Him; what He wanted to do through me was awesome. And so I gave Him my life to do with as He pleased: "Behold the handmaid of the Lord; be it unto me according to thy word."[25] These words would govern everything that happened to me for the rest of my life, and never would I regret my words.

Accountability. And then there were those who helped me make sure I would stay true to Him. My older cousin Eliza-

beth, who was also miraculously pregnant, shared her wisdom
and godliness and helped me form my own responses to what
was taking place in my life.[26]

So this is my message to you: God also has great plans
for you. He can always use small vessels like you and me, but
He can never use ones that have not been washed clean.[27]
He's looking for hearts that have been made pure with His
forgiveness. He's looking for those of you who have determined to follow His way, no matter what. To be ready for
what He has for you. To be faithful, humble, reverent, and
accountable. And to every day, all over again, turn over your
life to Him with words similar to mine: "Be it unto me according to thy word." When you do, you too can know that
God will look at you and say you're "highly favored" and
"blessed among women."[28] Your part is to receive His forgiveness and, out of gratitude, to remain pure and ready for His
use. His part is to use you.

God's richest blessings to you as you continue on this
journey,

Mary

Purity and You

As Mary told us, purity is a heart thing. Impure actions on the outside
of the body originate from an impure heart. Therefore, pure actions
can take place only when we have a pure heart. That's why the Bible
tells us, "Who may climb the mountain of the Lord? Who may stand
in his holy place? Only those whose hands and hearts are pure."[29]

Look at the truths that can set you free:

❋ *SHE Lives the Truth* ❋

1. Without God's power I can't resist temptation, but with His power I can.

Lie: It doesn't matter how much temptation I allow in my life, I can handle it.

Many married women think, *I'm married, so sexual purity messages
don't apply to me.* This kind of attitude is exactly what Satan wants us to

embrace, since he knows that just when we think we don't have an issue with something, we are most susceptible.

Scripture tells us, "Can a man scoop fire into his lap and not be burned? Can he walk on hot coals and not blister his feet?"[30]

Obviously the answer to both these questions is no. We are born into sin and that sin will hound us till the end of our life.

If you have chosen to live God's way, you are a marked target for Satan. He's out to destroy you by getting you to fall for his lies. The good news is, with Christ's power you have the victory because He loves you.[31] You *can* win over sexual temptation. You must be ready for it when it comes, recognize it for what it is, and have a strategy for escaping it.

> **LYNDA** ✳ When I was a single mom, my strategy for sexual purity included:
>
> > having someone to regularly hold me accountable;
> > steering clear of compromising situations;
> > refusing to watch or listen to things that ignited my passions;
> > turning my lonely, needy times into giving times—visiting the sick in the hospital or calling a hurting friend. ✳

Whether you're a single woman facing sexual pressure to compromise or a married woman facing temptation at work or an impure thought life at home, try this RUN acronym to help you stand strong:

Recognize the temptation for what it is.
Understand Satan's desire to destroy you—run from tempting situations.
Never return to that situation or mind game—rely on God's power through prayer to help you do this.

Always recognize the "grass-is-greener mentality," even while reading Christian novels, which can sometimes make us think, *I don't have it that good.* Watch what you read, and guard your thought life. Don't allow yourself to fantasize and commit the sin of lust. God created us to be sexual women and to enjoy sex within the healthy boundaries of marriage. He doesn't want us to see it as something dirty or a list of one hundred *don'ts*. He wants us to focus our goal for purity to one *do: Do* follow God's commands.

2. It's my job to talk to my kids about sex.

Lie: My kids don't need me to talk to them about sex; they hear about sex education at school.

Even though sex saturates our society, as parents we often fail to adequately teach our children about it—why God created it, how He intended it to work, and what happens when we don't follow His ways. Because of our discomfort in discussing the subject, our children turn to peers and the media to learn and ask questions. If we do talk to our kids about sex, too many times we base the discussion on the negatives. We teach the don'ts without helping them base the reasons on the One who created sex in the first place.

> **REBECCA** ✳ I did talk about purity with my mum and dad. From the time my siblings and I were very young, my parents fostered open communication with us. As a teen I felt that I could talk to them about everything, which is such a comfort at that very vulnerable, influential time of life. My parents were straight with us about the consequences of going against God's way. They also didn't just say, "Don't have sex outside of marriage," but "Here's why God says not to be involved in impurity." This not only made us respect them, but we listened to them too. ✳

> **LYNDA** ✳ I can't remember one conversation my parents had with me about sex. Their discomfort and awkwardness in talking with us about this topic transferred to me. Once while driving my then ten-year-old son, Clint, home from a doctor's appointment, I broached the topic of sex by talking about the horses he'd seen on his dad's farm and the breeding they'd done. Then I discussed God's design for sex and how natural and good it was within the wholeness of God's rules, and how relevant those rules would be for him in the days to come. I glanced down at my white knuckles holding the steering wheel as I asked, "Do you have any questions about sex?"
>
> "Yes," he said.
>
> *Rats,* I thought uncomfortably.

"What do mountain lions eat?" Clint asked.

I breathed a sigh of relief and ruffled his hair, secretly glad that I could delay the "big talk" with my son. I told him I was there when he did have questions, and if I didn't know the answers, I knew where to find them. In the years since, he has asked more questions, and my husband and I were there when he did. ✳

The Bible instructs us to "teach [the truths] to your children. Talk about them when you are at home and when you are away on a journey, when you are lying down and when you are getting up again."[32] That includes discussions about sex in natural, safe settings. Consult with older moms to find out effective ways they taught their children about sex. Check out books from the library to help you discuss the topic in age-appropriate ways. Use a Bible concordance to help you look up verses on purity together. And while you're discussing purity, remember to model it too. Guard what you see, say, and do, and that will be the loudest lesson of all to your kids.

3. I am responsible for dressing in a way that won't make a man's struggle for purity more difficult.

Lie: It doesn't matter what I wear. It is the guy's responsibility to control his lustful thoughts.

One of the ways that we as women can show our inner commitment to purity is through the way we dress.

REBECCA ✳ I once heard a simple talk from the mission director's wife at my church that greatly impacted me. She shared that some of the guys at church had complained that they didn't know where to look because of the way many of the girls dressed. It made me see that we have a responsibility to protect other Christians' eyes. ✳

Several good rules of thumb for our modesty—whether we're married or single—include:

✳ not too short
✳ not too tight
✳ not too much skin

If you don't trust your own conscience to decide what that means, ask an older woman or mentor (preferably one who has a good sense of style!).

4. I can be forgiven and set free from my sin.

Lie: I've sinned so much that I can never be pure again.

REBECCA ⁕ Forgiveness of self is essential when dealing with sexual purity. None of us has handled this area perfectly, and some of us have messed it up royally. Whatever your past consists of in this area, God can give you a new start. Whether you're married or single, when you go to Him, He can help you not only heal from the past, but He can send you into the future with new habits and a new determination to remain pure. ⁕

The Bible says, "If we confess our sins to him, he is faithful and just to forgive us and to cleanse us from every wrong."[33]

If you have unconfessed sin in your life, pray this prayer along with us:

Dear Lord, thank You for the gift of Your grace to me. I confess that I have hurt You by (name your sin/sins) _____

_____ .

I am so sorry, and I accept Your forgiveness. Thank You for Your promise that You won't remember my sins anymore. Help me to walk in purity in the days ahead and to run from temptation. In Jesus' name, amen.

In closing, let's consider the well-known story of Pinocchio. At one time, this little wooden boy enjoyed life with his creator, Geppetto. Then, despite his conscience telling him to stay away from temptation, he's lured into a new life that looks like a world of fun from the outside. But as he gets involved with those around him, not only does he begin changing into a donkey and getting led away from the real boy he wanted to be, he also desperately misses the joy of being with his father.

In the same way, when we give in to the temptation that looks like so much fun, we succeed only in allowing the tempter to rip us off. Our sin becomes a distracting, dividing wall between us and God, and we miss out on fellowship with Him. On top of this, we start the process of becoming a spiritual donkey—used and enslaved. The bottom line is, sin draws us further and further away from the SHEs we want to be.

Of course, the ending to the story of Pinocchio is a good one. He recognized the bad choices he had made and ran from them. He returned to Geppetto. Also, though undeserved on his part, he was graciously given his heart's desire and made into a real boy.

Do you see the hope for you and me?

✳ **SHEism** ✳ The truly pure SHE keeps her heart clean before God and enjoys the health of a pure mind and body.

Purity Covenant

A man named Job made this promise about his own sexual purity: "I made a covenant with my eyes not to look with lust upon a young woman" (Job 31:1).

I, _____, also want to make a covenant on this day, _____, to become and remain a pure woman:

✻ I commit to speak and act purely.

✻ I commit to dress modestly.

✻ I commit to take captive any impure or lustful thoughts.

✻ I commit to keep myself from watching, listening to, and looking at anything that would have a harmful impact on my mind and life.

✻ I commit to abstain from any form of sex outside of marriage.

✻ I will pray for God's power to remain true to this covenant. Amen.

Signed, _____

Additional Resource:

Rebecca St. James, **Wait for Me** (Nashville: Thomas Nelson, 2002)

"It is not easy to turn loose of old habits or resentment, but when I do, I am rewarded with a great sense of freedom, as though my spiritual 'closet' has been decluttered. And I can more easily find the good things of God that I'm seeking."

Barbara Johnson *The Women of Faith Devotional*[1]

> "If the Son sets you free, you will indeed be free."
> John 8:36

Free: Finding Emotional Healing

LYNDA ✳ I looked forward to my Tuesday afternoon appointment with a man I'll call Stephen, president of a large ministry in the United States. It was July 1998, and I had scheduled an interview time with him, as I had with many other authors, to obtain articles for *Single-Parent Family* magazine. I especially looked forward to my time with Stephen because he had counseled and mentored me in the past, and I couldn't wait to share what God had been teaching me. I just knew he would be amazed at my progress, overwhelmed at my vast spiritual growth since we had last met.

But such was not the case. I greeted Stephen warmly as he arrived in the room where I was conducting my interviews. We sat at a table opposite each another, and we updated each other on our lives. I don't remember my words to him, but I'll never forget his words to me: "Do you have another interview scheduled? If so, please change it. God has something He wants to do in your life today. You have some unforgiveness issues against your former husband that need to be taken care of once and for all."

Well, this wasn't exactly the reception I had imagined. Unforgiveness? Me? I had been on my own—and in ministry—for more than a decade. Single moms and dads all over the world looked up to me as their champion, as the voice of "their" magazine and two books I'd written addressing "their" issues. I was even scheduled to fly to Europe on Friday, the day after I returned home from a conference, to minister in Wales and Northern Ireland to single moms and dads through Care for the Family, a small ministry that conducts work similar to what Focus on the Family does in the United States.

Yet I had enough confidence in Stephen to do as he said. With my last afternoon appointment rescheduled, I took my place again across the table from him. He opened his Bible to Matthew 18:21-35 and read to me Jesus' story about an unforgiving servant who refused to forgive someone's debt, even though his master had just forgiven his own—even greater—debt. When the master heard of the man's refusal to forgive, he turned the servant over to be tortured. Stephen looked up at me then read the verse that connected the servant's story to mine: "So also My heavenly Father will deal with every one of you, if you do not freely forgive your brother from your heart his offenses."[2]

Stephen said, "You are being tormented in a prison of unforgiveness. The things that happened to you all those years ago still have their hold on you. You *must* forgive your ex-husband from your heart for his offenses or you will remain in bondage to him."

He had me name every act of betrayal my ex-husband had ever done to me. I had never verbalized some of the specifics, and others were so horrible that Stephen gasped. But with everything I said, he laid some object on the table—a paper clip, a pencil, a tissue. Then one by one he had me pick up the object, name the associated offense, pray to forgive, then let them go once and for all. This exercise hurt from deep inside me like nothing I had experienced before. I wept till I heaved. At times Stephen would stop me saying, "You're not there yet on that one," and I'd have to do the exercise again.

When we finished with everything I could think of, Stephen had me pray and ask God to reveal other issues that had lodged themselves in the unforgiveness portion of my heart. Stephen said, "Lynda, within thirty days, you will have taken five years off your countenance."

It was after six o'clock in the evening when he left, and the Anaheim Convention Center had closed for the day. It was quiet except for the sounds of people sweeping and emptying trash cans. I sat alone trying to soak in what had just happened to me. As I stood to gather my things, I couldn't help but remember the words of the song Larnelle Harris and Sandi Patty sing—"I've Just Seen Jesus." I knew that something life changing had happened to me.

I attended a reception later that night, still engrossed in what had occurred a few hours earlier. When I returned to my hotel room, I turned on my tape recorder to revisit the session. As with all my interviews, I had recorded this one and had checked the red light often to make sure it blinked with each sound of our voices. When I tried to play it back, however, I discovered that nothing had recorded.

I went to bed and prayed. "God, was this as real as I think it was?" With that question, I fell asleep. I dreamed I discovered a blemish on my face that had come to a head. When I touched it, a wire protruded from it that wound throughout the inside of my whole body. I felt like God was saying to me that the sore of unforgiveness had affected every part of me, and it had now come to a head. It was time to clean it out.

So began some open-heart surgery—emotional, that is. Complete healing didn't happen overnight. After all, I was dealing with years of pain, rooting out seeds of anger and bitterness that had coiled their thorny branches through my spirit. But in the weeks ahead, I felt their grip lessen.

One Friday night about six weeks later, my former husband called to talk with the children. I seized the opportunity to tell him about my experience and asked him to forgive my unforgiving behavior. He still wasn't a safe person, and *he* hadn't changed. But *I* was changed, and because of that, I had changed the situation. Today I have a good relationship with him and his wife, and I pray for them often.

You might be wondering, What's the big deal? Why was this such a huge event for you, Lynda?

My part in writing this book would have been much different on the other side of forgiveness. I've been able to go deeper in my post-forgiveness walk with God. I've been able to live out my faith to my former husband and his family since I made the decision to forgive. My children would be glad to tell you what a difference the change in me has made in our family life. And I'm especially thankful I met and married Dave *after* I forgave.

Forgiveness was such a huge event because it set me free. Forgiveness released me from

> bondage I didn't even know I was in;
> bondage I had become accustomed to;
> bondage that had grown to feel natural;
> bondage I'd come to accept would never change;
> bondage I didn't know was bondage. ✳

Independence Day

At first glance, freedom may not seem to be such a struggle for you. You may feel full of spiritual and emotional freedom. You may have even considered skipping this chapter. After all you live in a free country and in a free society. You're free to marry who you want and free to attend the college and church of your choice. You may see freedom only as removing unwanted physical restraints and a license to do as you please. . . . Or, like most of us, you may struggle with things that continue to keep you in bondage—things like fear, worry, insecurity, and addictions.

LYNDA ✳ Everyone encounters pain, disappointment, and heartache. Like many of you, I had had no trouble accepting the fact that Jesus died for my sins. I did, however, fail to accept the freedom God offered me even in the midst of hard stuff. Sometimes deliberately, sometimes ignorantly, I failed to get rid of the very things that prevented my freedom. I held on to, and even nurtured, much of my bondage through my "justified" responses, which kept me from finding the joy and peace Jesus promised.[3] ✳

Bondage is anything that keeps you from experiencing God's best for you. Are you living the abundant life? Are you really free? Here are ten questions to prompt your thoughts about your freedom:

* Do you struggle to let go of the past?

* Do you have trouble forgiving others, yourself, or God for certain things that have happened to you?

* Do you fear what might happen in the future?

* Do your goals, possessions, or relationships leave you wanting but never finding contentment?

* Do you allow one or more habits to control you?

* Do you ever lie or cheat?

* Do you often feel sad or depressed?

* Do you stay busy so you won't have to deal with hard issues?

* Do you resist quietness and alone time?

* Do you get mad easily?

If you answered yes to any of these questions, you might not be as free as you thought you were. Go back over the questions and list in your mind your problem areas. Do you want to be free from the things that still bind you?

LYNDA ✳ On my trip to Europe for Care for the Family following my forgiveness-freeing experience, I met with a woman I'll call Nancy, who had written to me from London to tell me how her pastor husband had betrayed her, lied to her, and ultimately left her for another woman—all while continuing to pastor and receive support from the congregation. I had sent her some books about dealing with grief and anger and some fun products for her kids from Focus on the Family. Then I made arrangements to meet her at a London train station upon my return from Paris. We hadn't been together long over dinner before it became apparent

Nancy also needed to deal with her hurts, so I tried to help her list on a sheet of paper some of the losses she'd suffered. Nancy stopped me and said she wasn't ready to face these things yet. But a letter arrived from her shortly after I returned home. She wrote, "Lynda, I didn't want you to go. You've learned to live life in color again, and I'm still living in black and white. Please help me. Show me how to change my life." ✲

At the beginning of this chapter, we mentioned Jesus' words: "You will know the truth, and the truth will set you free. . . . If the Son sets you free, you will indeed be free" (John 8:32, 36). When Jesus spoke these words, most people—including many who believed in Him—didn't realize He wanted to liberate their heart and unshackle everything that kept them from discovering the full life He came to bring them. Because they didn't see themselves in bondage, they also didn't see their need to be set free, so they missed out on the joy, peace, hope, and love He offered.

But Jesus wasn't talking about freedom as in human rights or freedom from oppression. It isn't the kind of freedom our nation's forefathers fought for. It's the kind our heavenly Father gave His Son to die for. It's the kind that asks us to hand over our rights to hold on to things and allow Him to give us back the kinds of freedoms that can never change or be taken away. It's the kind that faces the disappointments and heartbreaks life inevitably hands us and chooses to respond in the healthy and loving way that Jesus would. Jesus' kind of freedom offers strength to move past old hurts and healing for issues that continue to surface. His life brings health and wholeness and the promise of His love for always.

This chapter is about living life in color. It's about exchanging a black-and-white existence for a healthy life that radiates all the hues of Jesus' love.

> Jesus' life brings health and wholeness and the promise of His love for always.

Life is messy. There's no getting around that. We each have certain areas of our life in which Satan tries to attack us, put us in bondage, and limit—or destroy—our freedom. But even though we're all left with "stuff" to deal with from time to time, God can turn any roadblock into a doorway to freedom.

SHE finds health through God's freedom, and through that freedom, SHE can find true life filled with all the abundance and color that Jesus offers. Truth has been there all along, but each of us must know it, access it, and apply it to our own situation if we ever hope to find freedom and health.

> Jesus' kind of freedom offers strength to move past old hurts and healing for issues that continue to surface.

We're here to help you cash in on knowledge of God's truth—truth about the curses that cause bondage and the bigger truth about God's blessings that break curses and set you free.

The Truth about Curses

REBECCA ❋ One of the most unfree women I have ever known is a young woman I'll call Rachel. She learned how to relate to other people the only way her family had taught her—through anger and yelling matches. Seeing her pain, I tried many times to draw her out and encourage her to let go, but she pushed me away. After my several failed attempts to help her, she started to direct her bitterness toward me through hurtful words, silent treatment, and other behaviors she knew would get to me. It was as though she had admitted herself into a self-imposed prison, thrown away the key, and was purposely keeping people from finding it. The last I heard, my friend is still in that same angry, bitter place. ❋

We're all capable of holding on to our pain indefinitely when the idea of dealing with our issues seems more frightening than the safety and comfort of our grief. When we hold on to our issues, we not only hurt ourselves, but God and others around us as well. Every bondage has its root in some kind of curse. We don't hear curses talked about a lot from our pulpits, yet churches are full of people like you and me living with the consequences of them. Ignorance and shame keep us from acknowledging bondage for what it is. We fail to recognize the spiritual cause and effect because the lack of freedom has become so embedded in our day-to-day existence that we don't know any other way than living under its control. We've seen similar patterns passed down from generation to generation since Adam and Eve first sinned in the Garden of Eden.

A simple definition for *curse* as a verb is "to invoke evil on or afflict." The big curse happened to humankind in the Garden when Adam and Eve sinned. God pronounced the resulting curse on women:

> *You will bear children with intense pain and suffering. And though your desire will be for your husband, he will be your master.*[4]

Men also still deal with results of that first sin:

> *I have placed a curse on the ground. All your life you will struggle to scratch a living from it.*[5]

Within the big consequences that we all have to live with, the serpent, Satan, sees to it that smaller curses happen to us, so insidious that we don't see them as such. "Family baggage" we might call them. A family as small as a husband, wife, and children or a family as big as a church or even a country suffer the effects, often unknowingly.

Curses continue their destruction when they aren't recognized and broken. You might have opened a door yourself, or maybe the actions of someone in your family generations ago brought lingering trouble. If that describes your situation, you can put an end to it and cut off the pain of things like divorce, disease, alcohol, poverty . . . the list goes on. Unforgiveness, bitterness, inferiority, or anger will continue to strengthen their suffocating grip on present and future generations unless the root problem is dealt with. The cycle of bondage looks something like this:

Humankind Curses: Bondage Cycle

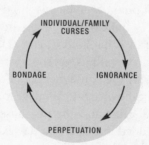

When old-man bondage takes control of us, our habits as well as our emotions become his. Discouragement, depression, dependency, and unhealthy desires become evidence of his presence. We become convinced that nothing's going to change, and we settle down to live as comfortably as possible within this bondage. Sadness, busyness, anxiety, feeling overwhelmed, and a whole host of other results become a part of life.

But there is another way. It's called freedom.

The Truth about Freedom

Being saved means we accept Christ as our personal Savior. *Saved* is the Greek word *sozo*, which means to be "completely whole." Not partially. Not only forgiven, but also healed, delivered, set free, and blessed. Romans 8:37 tells us, "Despite all these things, overwhelming victory is ours through Christ, who loved us."

Freedom means liberation from slavery or bondage or power from another. By recognizing the curse and by willfully exchanging individual rights for freedom to live within the guidelines God provides for us, we can break the hold that sin has over us and generations to come. But it takes intentional effort that won't quit.

So what about generational curses? Since they are real, don't they have a hold on us even as Christians and on our children after us? The Bible tells us that one man's sin will affect his children and his children's children for up to three or four generations.[6]

Yes, they do, unless we break their hold.[7]

When Jesus died on the cross, He took on the Curse for us—both the big curses and the individual curses. Our sin was heaped on Him. It died and was buried with Him. As a result, we can have new life in Him. We can be delivered from every curse and begin a fresh heritage of health and wholeness, bringing blessings to our family, church, city, and nation. Each of us now stands before God individually, no longer needing to be bound by the past. The only way a person can miss out on God's freedom is if she doesn't know the truth and apply it: "Do not snatch the word of truth from me, for my only hope is in your laws. . . . I will walk in freedom, for I have devoted myself to your commandments."[8]

The bad news is, curses are real even for a Christian. The good news is, Jesus' death made it possible to overcome anything. Curses can be broken and even reversed, but only for the Christian. Not only can we break generational curses, but we can reverse them and turn them into blessings.

> *Like a fluttering sparrow or a darting swallow, an unfair curse will not land on its intended victim.*[9]

By knowing this truth, we don't just have to ignore, perpetuate, and continue to live in bondage. Instead, we can recognize the curse, break and reverse its hold and control over us, and in the process find freedom and abundant life in Christ.

Humankind Curses: Bondage Cycle

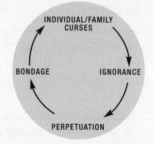

Humankind Curses: Freedom Cycle

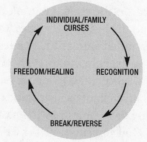

LYNDA ✳ One day when my son, Clint, was about eight, he got really mad at one of his sisters. He stomped the floor and said, "I just get my bad temper from . . ." and he went on to mention a member of his family.

With the words barely out of his mouth, I said, "Oh no you don't, Son." I sat him on the couch. The O. J. Simpson trial was going on at the time, so I pointed out that whether or not O. J. committed those atrocious murders, he had an uncontrollable temper problem that didn't just begin then. It started when he was three or five or seven and was left unchecked. I explained to Clint that when we are in Christ, we don't have to live out the curses that control us when we don't know Him, so we prayed for victory over that curse then and there.

I didn't see evidence of intense anger in Clint after that. One day when he was about thirteen, he came home from school and said, "Mom, I have a problem. I have to write a paper about the last time I got angry and lost my temper. I can't remember when the last time was."

What an opportunity to let my son measure both the power of generational curses and God's greater power over them. We recognized the curse, broke and reversed it, and now Clint walks free from something he didn't have to carry his whole life. He lives in freedom, not in bondage. He's learned to live life in color again.

So did Rahab. ✳

Rahab's Rehab (Joshua 2)

Rahab lived long before Jesus did, so she didn't know the rest of the story. But plenty happened before Jesus' time that hints of the incredible *sozo* work His death and resurrection would provide.

Rahab was an innkeeper, and she was also a prostitute. But who could condemn her? After all, she came from the evil Canaanite culture that generations earlier Noah had declared cursed.[10] This was Rahab's inheritance. Her apple hadn't fallen far from the tree. She had generations of excuses for her behavior. Nothing would ever change. Or would it?

We wonder what Rahab would have said if she'd realized her world—and the world of generations to follow—was about to change. Two spies from Israel had come to check out the city of Jericho because God had told Joshua, the Israelite leader, that He would conquer that city for them. Jericho was the key citadel of the Jordan valley, which lay between the Israelites and the Promised Land, so Joshua needed complete information about this fortress—its gates, its fortified towers, its military force, and the morality of its people. The Canaanite king heard about Joshua's two scouts and ordered their immediate capture. Rahab's home, perhaps the only place to lodge in such a small town, was built on a double city wall and was situated higher than other houses, so people couldn't see what occurred on her rooftop.[11] The men arrived at her place, and Rahab hid them on her secluded roof while the king's men searched on.

We wonder what made Rahab make an about-face that day. What caused her to turn her back on the only world she'd ever known and risk her life to trust these strangers? She admitted to them that the inhabitants of the land had witnessed their miracles and were fearful of them because of their God. She knew that the God of Israel had the power to free her of the bondage she and generations before her had been in. The buck of curses would stop with her. "Since I have saved your lives," she said to Joshua's men, "will you in turn save mine and those of my relatives?" Their answer? "Put a scarlet cord in your window."[12]

We wonder if, a few days later, Rahab saw the throng of Israelites march around the city walls in silent procession and continue for six days. On the seventh day, as the Israelites made their final trek around the city, Rahab heard the blast of trumpets before the Israelites began to shout. The earth trembled. The walls, which had safeguarded the city for years, crumbled and fell, leaving the city unprotected. But one wall remained erect—the wall where Rahab's house stood.

We wonder if Rahab knew her story wouldn't end with her choice to hang the scarlet cord. She had been a heathen woman in the bondage of past curses. But she seemed to realize there had to be more to life. Rahab broke the curse of sin by sparing the life of these men of God. She made the important choice to follow the God of Israel, but she wasn't content with just that. She wanted to be free and to free her family and generations to follow. She married one of Joshua's spies, and their descendants became part of the lineage of Jesus Christ. Talk about a new heritage!

We wonder if Rahab knew that *scarlet* means "twice dipped, double dyed, done twice." The scarlet cord stood as a simple reminder of her double-dipped blessing, which transformed her life of sin to one of forgiveness *and* freedom.

We wonder what Rahab would say if she'd heard Isaiah's prophesy, "Though your sins are like scarlet, they shall be as white as snow; though they are red as crimson, they shall be like wool."[13]

We wonder what she would say if she'd known that the One who would follow in her bloodline would shed His scarlet blood to wash away the sins of all humankind?

Freedom and You

We wonder what Rahab would say to you and me today if she were sitting in front of us, examining the curses and bondages we've gotten used to living with. She appears in the Hebrews 11 Hall of Faith: "It was by faith that Rahab the prostitute did not die with all the others in her city who refused to obey God. For she had given a friendly welcome to the spies."[14] We wonder if she would say:

✱ "You don't have to live with those curses."

✱ "Don't be one of those who doesn't believe or doesn't recognize."

✱ "Don't put God in a box. Don't underestimate His power to break even generations of bondage."

We wonder.

If you've accepted Jesus' gift of salvation, you've been washed clean through the blood He shed: You're double-dipped. Forgiven as well as free. On your way to heaven, but also able to live a free and holy life here on earth.

We can break the hold of anger, violence, drugs, depression—or anything else that binds us—right now. We don't have to wait!

God is the burden remover and the chain breaker. But standing around holding the keys of truth from God's Word won't open anything. We must stick the right key in the lock and open the door by praying,

"God, forgive me of my sins and break their power in my life. I have the keys to Your truths that free me from the curses that leave me in

bondage. I want the blessing instead of the curse. I want to replace the lies with truth."

Let's begin the freedom process right now.

---------------------------- ✳ *SHE Lives the Truth* ✳ ----------------------------

1. Freedom is mine for the taking.

Lie: I've just got to wait and let God drop freedom into my lap.

LYNDA ✳ I thought I'd done all I could to let go of the things that had been done to me, and I'd just have to live with things as they were. But like charcoals I once threw away because I'd mistakenly thought they'd grown cold, these issues and the bitterness I felt toward my former husband reignited with the slightest wind of disappointment, discouragement, or dismay. I didn't know I could do more to forgive other than say the words I had often said: "I choose to forgive him." I didn't know that the ropes of unforgiveness still bound me. I didn't know that a better, freer life was possible for me. I just didn't know. ✳

But now you know freedom is available. And knowing it's available is the first step in achieving it.

REBECCA ✳ I met Anna during a songwriting session at a record label where she worked. When Anna offered to help, I was immediately drawn to her joyful spirit. Over lunch one day soon after we'd met, we began to connect because of our relationship with God. She later shared with me that she had been the victim of sexual abuse at the hand of her cousin. But instead of perpetuating this bondage, Anna broke free. She exuded such an infectious joy, I would have never guessed she had dealt with such tragedy in her life. I have watched her give her pain to God and work through her past with the help of wise believers, and as she does, her freedom continues to grow. Anna taught me that freedom is possible, no matter what blows life has dealt you. ✳

Get out a pen and paper and list the areas of bondage in your own life. When you're finished, hold the list in your hands, and lift it to God in prayer. Name each area of bondage individually, and ask for His help in freeing you. In doing this, you have taken your first step in your freedom walk. We'll show you more to do in truth 4.

2. God can restore to me what Satan has stolen.

Lie: What I've lost can't be restored, so I'll always live in defeat.

Not only can God break the curse, He can restore what it has stolen from us.

> **LYNDA** ✳ I watched God restore to my family what was stolen through a divorce. ✳

> **REBECCA** ✳ I saw God bring hope and restoration to my heart after experiencing near burnout, which robbed me of my joy, my passion for ministry, and my enthusiasm for life.

> **REBECCA AND LYNDA** ✳ We didn't believe the lie that there was no light at the end of the tunnel. Instead, we believed that God could and would heal us. ✳

There's a story in the Bible of a king named Balak, who sent for a soothsayer to curse God's people. That curse didn't happen. Instead, God blessed them.[15] In the same way, what was meant for harm in your life can be turned around and used for good. Over and over in the Bible, God brought people from weakness and despair to a place of hope. He can do the same for us today when we surrender ourselves and our hurts, bondage, and burdens to Him in prayer.

> What was meant for harm in your life can be turned around and used for good.

Here are some wonderful verses to memorize that you can remind yourself of when you think you'll never recover from the losses of your life:

Proverbs 6:31: *But if [the thief] is caught, he will be fined seven times as much as he stole.*

Joel 2:25, NIV: *I will repay you for the years the locusts have eaten.*

3. There are steps I can take to find freedom.

Lie: I don't know how to be free.

To get rid of the curse or bondage, we have to admit we have a problem. We can no longer blame everyone or everything else. The curse stops here. It is important you understand the origins of *why* you're doing something (such as generational curses), but it doesn't excuse you that you *are* doing it. We're each responsible for the choices and decisions we make. Circumstances may have robbed you of your past; don't let them rob you of your future. The day of accepting responsibility has come. The day of covering up and making excuses is over. The day of being set free has arrived.

The Bible tells us that many of our battles can be won only with spiritual weapons through prayer.[16] Memorize these Scriptures and take the following steps to break the curses and find freedom in each area of your life:

REPENT.

Wait quietly before God. Let Him tell you the things you need to repent of. Ask Him to forgive you for whatever sin has stood between you and His best (e.g. anger, fear, or unforgiveness; sex, drugs, or alcohol addictions).

> 1 John 1:9: *If we confess our sins to him, he is faithful and just to forgive us and to cleanse us from every wrong.*

REFUSE TO LET THINGS GO ANY FURTHER.

When you yield control of any part of your life to anyone other than God, you give your permission to be attacked with destructive thoughts, temptations, and responses. It's time to put a stop to them and turn over the controls to God.

> 2 Corinthians 2:10-11: *I do so with Christ's authority . . . so that Satan will not outsmart us. For we are very familiar with his evil schemes.*

RESIST THE LIES OF SATAN.

Ed Silvoso of Harvest Ministries defines a stronghold as "a mind-set, impregnated with hopelessness, that causes us to see as unchangeable something that is contrary to God's Word."[17] The stronghold of lies Satan builds in your heart and mind can't be destroyed by your own strength. Pray in the name of Jesus Christ that you will no longer fall for these lies.

> 2 Corinthians 10:4: *We use God's mighty weapons, not mere worldly weapons, to knock down the Devil's strongholds.*

BELIEVE THE TRUTH.
Tear down satanic strongholds and use the bricks to build a tower of truth. This means reprogramming your mind with the Bible's truths about yourself, God, and Satan. When the enemy comes at you with intruding thoughts, flee to the truth tower.

> Proverbs 18:10: *The name of the Lord is a strong fortress; the godly run to him and are safe.*

TRAIN YOUR MIND TO THINK FREE AND HEALTHY THOUGHTS.
The mind is the battleground of spiritual warfare between God and Satan. Daily surround yourself with people, music, Bible reading—whatever it takes to keep your eyes on God's truths and the freedom He offers.

> Romans 12:2: *Let God transform you into a new person by changing the way you think.*

Reach out for accountability. Ask for advice from a godly person you respect. Ask her to hold you up in prayer and keep you accountable as you practice living in the freedom God has given you. Maybe the internal issues you face need specialized help. A Christian counselor from your church or local area could greatly help you find freedom from bondage. What a comfort to know that God has given us the church community to help us along as we walk through life together with Him. We are not alone as we journey toward absolute freedom!

It's time to live life in color.

REBECCA ✳ A twenty-eight-year-old woman named Heather Williams typifies the free SHE woman. Born into a home filled with neglect and abuse, she was dropped off a two-story balcony by her father when she was an infant. When she was eleven, her mother planned to hand her off to the state, but instead she was taken in by her grandfather. Five years later, an aunt and uncle legally adopted Heather, who by that time had become a rebellious young woman making choices she'd later regret.

Things began to change when she was eighteen. Her father, who had become a Christian, reentered her life and took her to church. There she heard of the grace-filled love of Jesus. Having searched everywhere else, desperate for real love, Heather surrendered her heart to Him. She began a new life and started to experience freedom from a past that had haunted her. In her words, she is now a "completely different person."

I met Heather years later at a concert of mine that her husband had helped to organize. At the time, she had just experienced the greatest tragedy of her life. After four years of trying to conceive, Heather and her husband, Tim, received a gift—a seemingly healthy boy named Caedmen. However, doctors discovered too late that his heart was twice the size of a normal infant heart.

Heather and Tim lost their baby boy only six months into his short life. Yet the joy that Heather showed despite her loss was inspiring to me. In her pain, she chose to turn to God instead of away from Him. She told me that many times she had prayed, "Lord, I don't want my son to be gone, but I trust You." She didn't try to act like everything was okay, but instead she shared her pain with those around her and especially with God. She said to me, "If you allow yourself to be consumed with your problem, you'll never get to the purpose God has for you."

During the painful months following Caedmen's death, Heather's husband felt God give him a promise: Not a year would go by before he held another child of his own in his arms. On Christmas Day that same year, just five days prior to the one-year anniversary of Caedmen's death, a healthy baby girl was born to Heather and Tim. Skye Caitlyn had entered the world, and God had granted the desires of a faithful woman's heart.

As a Christian, Heather did not allow the hard, painful experiences in her life to put her in bondage. Instead, she trusted in the truth of God's Word and His love for her. Now, that same truth frees her and colors her world. ✳

✳

✳ **SHEism** ✳ A truly free SHE has submitted to the power of God to free her from all bondage.

Additional Resources:

Neil Anderson, **The Bondage Breakers**, second ed. (Eugene, Ore.: Harvest House Publishers, 2000)

Cynthia Heald, **Becoming a Woman of Freedom** (Colorado Springs: NavPress, 1992)

Cynthia Spell Humbert, **Deceived by Shame, Desired by God** (Colorado Springs: NavPress, 2001)

Part Three
EMPOWERED

> "A heritage is not a heritage unless it is passed on from one generation to another. The work of God in your life has left you with a wealth of knowledge and experience—a treasured heirloom just waiting to be passed along."
>
> **Betty Huizenga** *Gifts of Gold: Gathering, Training, and Encouraging Mentors*[1]

A LEGACY OF LOVE
By Rebecca St. James

You have walked with me

My mentor friend,

You have lent me your listening ear

You have shared with me, you have understood

You have laughed with me through the years.

You who have lived before me,

Who have felt my pain, my fears,

I have cried upon your shoulder

Knowing that you, too, cried these tears.

You who sometimes learned the hard way

Your stories you have shared

Then I following along behind you

From wayward paths have been spared.

The years have flown,

I'm a mentor now

Passing on your pearls from above

I praise God for you my mentor friend

For you have left . . .

A legacy of love.

"As iron sharpens iron, a friend sharpens a friend."

Proverbs 27:17

Chapter 8

Mentored: "Will You Walk with Me?"

REBECCA ✳ Growing up in Australia, I recall that my parents' record collection included a few albums by a smiling, petite blonde named Evie. I'll never forget some of her song lyrics, such as "I'm only four feet eleven but I'm going to heaven" and "Come on ring those bells, light the Christmas tree." I didn't know that twenty years later, God would use this little lady to make a profound impact on my life.

My parents had become acquainted with Evie when she had toured in Australia. Because of that connection, she and her husband, Pelle, came to our shows whenever we were in Florida close to where they live. Each time I saw Evie, she would encourage me both personally and in my ministry. I felt a kindred spirit with her. Our personalities, love for God, and zest for life connected us. This bond was accentuated by the fact that she had walked where I was walking as a woman in the spotlight of Christian music. She understood me.

Over a period of time, I had become increasingly aware of my need for a mentor. I'd watched countless Christian artists lose their passion for ministry and become jaded, hurt, and hardened by what they had experienced because of the consistent barrage of physical, emotional, and spiritual demands to meet schedules and expectations. As a performer there is also pressure to become overly entertainment focused, proud, self-absorbed, and money hungry. I wanted to stay soft before God and as a woman. I didn't want my profession to cripple me as a person.

After one specific visit with Evie, I felt a particular desire to ask her to mentor me. I longed to sit at her feet and absorb her wisdom. She had such a Jesus joy in her life, and I respected her so much. I saw Evie as someone who'd been through everything I was going through and yet had maintained a glowing, radiant love for Jesus that I wanted too.

I prayed about the idea over the months to come, but I hesitated in asking her, not knowing what her response would be. Finally, one weekend early the next year, I sent Evie an e-mail expressing my desire. The following day, she called to say that she "just happened" to be visiting Nashville where I live, which I now know to be a rare occurrence, and she asked if we could get together that night. I was so excited to see God so obviously confirm that this mentoring relationship was right.

In her Opryland Hotel room, Evie and I talked, shared, and began what is now one of the most treasured relationships of my life. I had found my mentor. ❋

Female Friendships

In this book, the subject of mentoring is part of the *E* in SHE, which stands for the empowerment we can have through God. As we stated in chapter 1, God's kind of empowerment means He's the One who invests, authorizes, and equips us. And one of the ways He does that is through other people—godly mentors, who take the time to teach us things they've already learned. The Bible says it like this: "You have heard me teach many things that have been confirmed by many reliable witnesses. Teach these great truths to trustworthy people who are able to pass them on to others."[2]

REBECCA ✳ The apostle Paul taught Timothy, who taught other faithful believers, who taught others. Someone taught Evie. Evie teaches me what she has learned. I teach others what I have learned, and they teach others what they've learned. That's the godly mentoring model. ✳

Yet mentoring is a word most of us have heard of but know little about. We hear we're supposed to have a mentor, but we don't know where to find one. We know we're probably meant to be a mentor ourselves, but the very idea scares us to death.

What about you? Has mentoring been a part of your life? Or do you sometimes feel . . .

✳ unimportant and unworthy to have someone invest in your life?

✳ alone in your journey or abandoned by people you have looked up to?

✳ rejected in your attempts to reach out for help?

✳ overwhelmed with the tasks you've been given with seemingly no instruction on how to accomplish them?

✳ shackled with too much on your plate or too many mistakes of your own to be telling others how to live?

If you answered yes to any of these questions, then you've experienced firsthand both the need women have for mentors and the struggles we face in finding and being them. In this chapter, we want to show the value of mentoring and provide insights on how to both find a mentor and become one.

Previous generations found mentoring to be more commonplace. True, life was simpler and slower-paced. But whether mentors were talked about or not, everybody knew they needed them. People

learned how to grow into their role as a wise man or woman by learning at the feet of other wise men and women. They learned how to be
parents from those who'd already parented. They learned their trade
from experts willing to share their expertise. They learned how to
avoid certain pitfalls in life by those who'd managed to navigate their
way through.

An individualistic society took care of all that, however. Mentoring has been replaced with mantras of the day such as: "I'll do it my
way." "Who are you to tell me what to do?" "I'll do whatever feels
right."

We have forgotten we're social beings in need of other social beings. Homes and families are so splintered and fragmented that we
often don't take time to help those coming behind us. Unfortunately,
to some degree mentoring within the church family has similarly
fallen by the wayside. We don't hear often enough about the vital role
mentoring plays in our spiritual and emotional growth. We've forgotten that godly people depend on other godly people to become godly
people.

The word *mentor* comes from mythology. When the Greek war-
rior Odysseus went off to fight in the Trojan War, he left his young
son, Telemachus, in the care of a trusted guardian named Mentor. The
war lasted ten years, and it took another ten years for Odysseus to return home. When he did, he found his son had grown into a fine man
under the guidance of Mentor.

> We've forgotten that godly people depend on other godly people to become godly people.

From its Greek beginnings till now,
mentoring continues to be important. Some of today's most well-known Christian books define a
mentor like this:

> "*Someone who fundamentally affects and influences the
> development of another, usually younger person.*"[3]
>
> **Howard Hendricks**

> "*Someone who provides modeling, close supervision on special
> projects, individualized help in many areas—discipleship,
> encouragement, correction, confrontation, and a calling to
> accountability.*"[4]
>
> **Ted Engstrom**

"A trusted friend. . . . There must be a confidence in our relationships with the younger women, a trust that our sharing is sacred. Trust is built week by week as you meet together, laugh and learn together." [5]
Betty Huizenga

Like Huizenga, we also believe that mentoring involves a deep friendship. For purposes of this chapter and to describe one of the ways SHEs become empowered, we will simply define Christian mentoring as "a female friendship that involves one woman helping another woman become the person God designed her to be." The mentor's goal is to be a sounding board, to offer insights about life and faith, and to lead the mentee in a growing relationship with God so she can both manage her own life and become empowered to mentor someone else. And the mentee's goal is to be teachable and pliable.

* Mentoring means assisting, not fixing.

* Mentoring means guiding, not telling.

* Mentoring means walking alongside, not lording over.

* Mentoring means looking forward, not back.

* Mentoring means growing past hurts, not rehashing them.

* Mentoring means learning to depend on God through someone else, not depending on that someone else.

* Mentoring means capitalizing on our God-given strengths, not focusing on our weaknesses.

LYNDA * In *The Hungry Heart*, I introduced readers to a woman named Isabel whom I was privileged to mentor. It started with my invitation to take her to lunch one day. I had stayed in touch with her since she'd come to faith in Christ some three years before. Our lunch consisted of Isabel's tears and explanations of the hardships in her life. Our lunch ended with my question to her, "Isabel, what happens if you don't eat? You grow weak, you can't do your work, and you cease growing.

You need someone to come along beside you and help you eat spiritual food so you can succeed in other areas of your life as well."

We started meeting over her lunch hour on Thursdays. At first, I had her read portions of the Bible, starting with Philippians. We talked, applied Scripture to her circumstances, and prayed. Now some two years later, another woman has joined our Thursday lunchtime. We often use Cynthia Heald's Bible studies, but every week the Holy Spirit takes over the agenda. These studies are extraspecial because Cynthia has taken the time to mentor me from a distance, and I get the opportunity to pass it on. These two women have grown and learned to apply God's truths to their daily lives. They've even started helping others. As for me, I've grown, too, and never have I done anything that I feel is so quietly pleasing to God.

This mentoring project is long-term; others are short. Ours doesn't involve a set curriculum; some do. Ours is informal; others are more planned. Ours works out well; others don't. The circumstances surrounding mentoring are as varied as the people who participate in these relationships. One thing is certain, though: A mentor is someone all of us, regardless of age or stage in life, need to both *get* and *become*. ❊

Finding a Mentor

LYNDA ❊ Tina is another woman I've known who has quite a story. Her mother was a prostitute and drug addict who left her at birth in the hospital. Tina's grandmother raised her till she was in her early teens. After her grandmother died, Tina went to live with her other relatives, where a male family member started molesting her. Soon, Tina had a boyfriend, and when she became pregnant, she didn't know if the baby belonged to the boyfriend or the family member. She moved into another relative's house, and soon after, her boyfriend was killed.

I knew Tina for a few years, beginning when her daughter was about twelve. During that period, Tina lived with three different guys and sent her daughter to live with at least two different families. I lost track of them a few years ago, so I don't know the rest of their story, but I wonder about them often. Never have I seen a more classic example of someone without anyone to show her how to make better, more deliberate and informed decisions.

Imagine what would have happened if Tina had allowed me or someone else to show her how to be a godly woman and mother. Imagine the abuse and wrong choices that could have been prevented. Imagine how life would have been different for her daughter and grandchildren.

The lesson her story impressed on me reminds me of a cross-country race I watched my son run one rainy Saturday in the fall of his senior year in high school. At six feet three and 155 pounds, his lanky, long-legged build gave him his usual advantage. The gun sounded and off they went. The cold morning rain created adverse conditions for the race, as did the difficult trail. Clint was in the lead, and as he approached a fork in the path, he agonized over which way to go. He looked around for someone to help him, to point out the right path, but found no one. So he made his best choice on his own and completed the race. He crossed the finish line in first place, but he soon discovered he'd taken the wrong turn. Not only had he run the wrong path, but all those behind him had too. So the race had to be disqualified from the season record.

Once again, imagine the different race I'd be reporting if someone had been there to point the way? When Clint's pathway wasn't clear, challenging conditions added more trouble, and his past experiences were inadequate, he could have used the advice from someone who'd been there before and knew the right path.

Just as Clint could have blamed a lack of coaching for his mistake, a lot of people blame their poor choices on their past, their bad family background, or their lack of mentors. But we have the Bible as a map that lays out the course for us as well as access to mature Christians in churches and ministries who can help show us the way to go. Even if we don't naturally inherit good guidance from our family, we can find guidance through mentoring. ✴

REBECCA ✴ I discovered with Evie that finding a mentor works best when it is need driven. Success is most likely to happen when the mentee asks for mentorship from someone who has had a similar—though not identical—life experience. For example, an experienced mother I know is mentoring three people, two of whom came to her out of a need for wisdom in mothering.

Another effective mentoring partnership I know of involves a young, recently widowed twenty-five-year-old woman who is processing her grief and her "whys" with an older woman who also lost her husband at a young age. ✳

LYNDA ✳ During my days with *Single-Parent Family* magazine, the most common plea I heard from single moms and dads around the world was, "Please, help my children and me find mentors!" When I would do a radio interview, I'd often receive calls from single parents saying, "The church isn't helping me," followed by calls from church leaders saying, "We want to help but we don't know how." Major disconnect. Where do we begin finding mentors? What qualities do we look for? It isn't as difficult as we sometimes make it out to be. You may already be in a natural mentoring relationship—either giving or receiving. An awesome mentoring possibility might be right under your nose. ✳

Becoming a Mentor

LYNDA ✳ I used a ministry-in/ministry-out model to encourage single parents. We've already established that all of us need mentors, but a woman raising her children alone becomes even more aware of this truth. Ministry-in happens when a single mom—or any of us—finds someone to walk alongside in our journey. Ministry-out, however, is just as important. I hadn't been a single mom long when my children and I started volunteering at an inner-city ministry through our church. That experience helped us reach outside our own needs and into the needs of others. In turn, ministry-out aided in our healing. ✳

We have a tendency to look through a straw at the issues we face today and at our search for someone to help us address those needs. When we dare to give the challenges to God and take the straw from our eyes, we'll be able to notice people all around us in need. God wants to use you in a unique way in someone else's life, and He can provide all you need to follow His lead. He asks only for your willingness to trust Him with the concerns in your life. When you do that, there's no limit to what He can do in and through you.

Finding someone to mentor may not be necessary: God can bring her to you. Ask God to provide the people He wants you to influence. Then watch! They'll come out of the woodwork—for both short- and long-term mentoring. It could happen in a brief moment at the grocery store, during a two-hour conversation on a plane, or over several years with someone in the singles or young-marrieds groups in your church. Others are praying for what you have. You'll start noticing God-appointments throughout your day—noncoincidental encounters. When you throw your heart into helping others, ministry-out will become one of the most rewarding experiences you could ever have.

Naomi and Ruth: Biblical Mentoring 101 (Ruth 1–4)

History provides a great example of mentoring in Ruth, one of only two books of the Bible called by a woman's name. Ruth actually means—guess what?—"friendship" or "female friend." The surface theme of this book sums up all we've talked about so far about female friendship—or mentorship—between an older and younger woman. The second and foundational theme is something much bigger. Almost every commentator says the book of Ruth is a snapshot of the sovereignty and mercy of God, which brings a joyful end to a story that begins with famine, death, and loss. Let's see what they mean.

Theme One: Female Friendship
Setting:
Naomi and her husband had moved with their two sons from Bethlehem to the evil nation of Moab to escape a famine.
Both sons married Moabite women.
Characters:
Naomi and her husband
Ruth and Orpah, daughters-in-law
Boaz, relative of Naomi's husband
Conflict:
All three women had become widows. Naomi prepared to move back to Bethlehem. Would Ruth and Orpah go with her,

when their chances of finding security in a new husband were far greater in Moab?

Action:

Ruth accompanied Naomi back to Bethlehem, where she found a job gleaning in the fields. She didn't know that her boss, Boaz, was a distant relative of Naomi's husband.

Core Truth:

The relationship between Naomi and Ruth empowered both of them to grow as God's women and to fulfill their unique calling.

Resolution:

Boaz and Ruth married and had a son, Obed. . . .

Theme Two: Redeemer Relationship

God brought Naomi and Ruth together and used their relationship to accomplish His incredible plans. Let's look at the situation.

If Naomi had had another son, she could have relied on him for support after her husband died. In addition, that son would have acted as *kinsman-redeemer*, marrying Ruth to ensure her future and to continue the family line. One could see the kinsman-redeemer as a rescuer. However, Naomi had run out of sons to rescue her daughters-in-law, leaving the two women on their own in a culture that wasn't kind to widows.

Yet they weren't alone. God used Boaz to be the kinsman-redeemer, who could save the women from harm and destitution. Boaz illustrates Jesus, who became mankind's Kinsman-Redeemer through His death, and who makes things right between God and anyone who trusts Him for salvation. The parallel looks like this:

Naomi/Ruth ————————————▶ Boaz (kinsman-redeemer)

Female friendships ——————————▶ God (Kinsman-Redeemer)

Naomi and Ruth's female friendship led Ruth to Boaz, who became her kinsman-redeemer. In the same way, godly mentoring relationships can point us to Jesus, our Redeemer. Just as God works through our regular circumstances, the seemingly ordinary events in the book of Ruth, such as travels, marriages, deaths, and harvests, as well as sleeping, eating, and purchasing land, revealed the rescuing, guiding activity of a loving God who takes personal care of those who trust their life to Him. Despite all appearances to the contrary, the faithful God had been about His business on Ruth's behalf. The icing on the cake was that she became part of the lineage of Jesus Christ. Ruth and Boaz's son, Obed, became the grandfather of David, who was in the direct line of Christ. Ruth lifted her eyes from her own min-istry-in needs to the bigger picture of ministry-out. When she made that decision, she had no idea how God would use her to bless all generations to come.

The same Providence that directed Ruth to the appropriate Bethlehem field later led the magi to that same town to see the Savior.[6] A mile east of Bethlehem stands that "field of Boaz," which is known as the spot where Ruth gleaned ears of corn. The field next to it is called the "field of the shepherds." Tradition holds that the angels first proclaimed Christ's birth over that spot.[7] In the place where Ruth and Boaz met, more than a thousand years later, angels sang, "Glory to God in the highest, and on earth peace among men with whom He is pleased."[8]

And God used the friendship of women to accomplish His plan.

Mentoring and You

Naomi and Ruth didn't know that we'd still be talking about their friendship thousands of years later and, in fact, using it as a model to establish female friendships of our own. But here we are. Naomi and Ruth could have believed the lies that nothing would ever be any dif-ferent, remained in Moab, gone their separate ways, and never have had the opportunity to see the results their friendship would pro-duce.

Are your eyes lifted to the bigger picture? Do you have a more mature female in your life who helps you do this? God can also use female friendships to usher you into your part of what the future holds before Jesus comes back. But as with Naomi and Ruth, your new mentored life can begin by applying these five truths:

1. My mentor teaches from her experiences, including her mistakes, and I grow from the wisdom she's learned.

Lie: A mentor must be perfect and have everything together, so I'll never find one or be one.

When Naomi moved with her husband from Bethlehem to Moab, they probably were outside of God's plan because Moab was a heathen nation. But despite their mistakes, God created an opportunity to demonstrate His grace to Naomi, which she passed on to Ruth. In what ways might God be redeeming you? Could it be that God wants to use a mentor/mentee relationship to help redeem you from your past?

> **LYNDA** ✳ I have used my experience of a failed marriage to help mentor many young women. Not only has God forgiven my mistakes, but He has used them to help me speak with passion and mercy from my heart to other women struggling with marriage or divorce. All of us have made mistakes. Understand and use them in both finding and becoming a mentor. ✳

The godly woman you choose for your mentor should have a genuine heart both for you and for the art of mentoring. She should be willing to sacrifice time and energy and be willing to commit for the long haul. She should be a woman of deep integrity and one who will keep the content of your times together confidential. She should demonstrate wisdom, patience, and both emotional and spiritual maturity. (Age is not all that matters.) Howard Hendricks says a mentor

✳ seems to have what you personally need;

✳ cultivates relationships;

✳ is respected and consulted by other Christians;

❊ offers a network of resources;

❊ talks as well as listens;

❊ demonstrates a mature and consistent lifestyle;

❊ can diagnose your needs;

❊ shows concern with your interests.[9]

Keep these qualities in mind as you keep your eyes open for a mentor. Perfection is not required, but maturity is. Your mentor doesn't keep making the same mistakes; she learns from them and uses them to make her wise and then to teach you.

2. I need to first build a relationship with the woman who mentors me.

Lie: Mentoring is about sharing personal things with someone I barely know.

Naomi developed an ordinary relationship with Ruth and Orpah first. We see evidence of their relationship when Naomi tried to say good-bye to them. Naomi kissed them, they cried, the younger girls offered to go with her, and Naomi called them "my daughters" three times. Later we see how Orpah kissed Naomi, and Ruth "clung to her."[10]

Naomi was mentoring long before she was seen as such. She mentored in ordinary ways in natural settings while the girls were married to her sons. Then when things got tough, the girls responded lovingly to Naomi.

REBECCA AND LYNDA ❊ Both of us have been profoundly impacted by mentoring from our mothers. Even if you didn't experience mentoring in your childhood home, you can both find a good mentor and be one as an adult. Start where you are with those women who are in your everyday life. Some may develop into a full-blown friendship; some may not. Just remember that you are a possible mentor to everyone you encounter or who is observing your life. Don't force it to happen or resist it when it does. Just let God shine His love through you no matter how long the duration may be, so when other women go through tough times, they'll want what you have. ❊

3. The mentor God has for me knows Him in an intimate way, and she encourages me to seek God intimately as well.

Lie: As long as she is a Christian, it doesn't really matter who mentors me.

Not just any older woman will do as your mentor. God is busy choosing someone—or someones—who are growing in intimacy with Him. Naomi obviously had developed her relationship with God at earlier times, so she knew where to turn when she faced hard times.

> **REBECCA** ∗ I believe that we each need to ask God to show us who He would have to mentor us. If I had just randomly picked a lady from my church without asking God to provide for me, my mentor-mentee relationship would not be the joyous, truly blessed friendship it is with Evie. The two of us share intimacy with Jesus and an understanding of each other that only He could have orchestrated. ∗

Once you're sure you desire a godly mentoring relationship and know what you want from it, try these "mentor getters":

∗ Pray for a mentor.

∗ Write out specifics of your wants and needs.

∗ Ask your church leaders for recommendations and referrals.

∗ Keep your eyes open for someone who exemplifies the traits you desire.

∗ Call the woman you've watched and admired. Ask for an appointment to see her about a specific issue. Use a go-between to set up a meeting if it feels more comfortable.

∗ Don't mention the word *mentor* until you see if that's where God takes you.

∗ Get to know her better to see if God might be leading you to this particular woman.

* Ask her advice about a specific challenge you're facing or clarity on a Scripture you've read.

* Inquire about her mentors and other women she has helped.

* Remember, some of the best mentors are those who don't formally see themselves as such. Wisdom is better than titles, and God has someone really wise and special just waiting for you.

The most important thing to remember in finding a mentor is that it is God's design. The Bible calls one person helping another person to live a wise and godly life iron sharpening iron.[11] Because passing on eternal truths is part of God's plan for others to sharpen you, praying for that to happen within your friendships is God's will. The Holy Spirit will guide you. He already has begun by having you read this chapter.

4. My mentor will help me see God at work and help me move beyond the past as I learn to grow in a healthy way.

Lie: No one can help me.

Return is a key word in the book of Ruth. Naomi reversed the direction she and her husband had taken. She turned away from Moab and the errors of the past. She left the tragic graves of her loved ones and headed back to Judah, her homeland. She also helped Ruth focus on the future and where they'd go from there.

God *always* uses bad and good things to show His love and glory when we hand over our concerns to Him. One of the key goals of the female friendship is to keep our eyes focused on what lies ahead, glancing at the past and what it has to teach us, then concentrating on the future and the ways God might use us to bring Him glory.

REBECCA * One of the things I've enjoyed in my times with Evie is that we can laugh and cry together; we can share the joys and the sorrows. With Evie, I can completely be myself, let my hair down. With her, I'm not Rebecca St. James—I'm just Rebecca. That's the kind of person we all need as a mentor: someone with whom we can

truly be ourselves. The point is, difficulties are a part of life and something we need to be honest about with our mentors and mentees; but
we must also work past our difficulties together to a place of healing
and ultimately empowerment. ❋

The benefits you gain from having a mentor and the degree to
which she can help you move forward depend on you. Just as
mentoring relationships are defined and constructed differently, they
also provide for different needs. Ask for the Holy Spirit's guidance as
you customize the relationship to fit your desires. What do you need
from your mentoring relationship?

❋ prayer support

❋ wisdom

❋ encouragement

❋ a sounding board without condemnation

❋ experience

❋ a networker

❋ a provider of biblical truth

❋ vision, or eyes to see the bigger picture

The one thing having a mentor should not do is keep you stuck.
Instead, her role is to help you become healthy, vibrant, and growing.
How that happens and specific areas *where* that happens depend on
your needs and desires. Decide what you want from a mentoring relationship, then with prayerful direction from God, go out and find
one.

5. I don't have the time *not* to mentor and be mentored.

Lie: I don't have the time or the energy to mentor and be mentored.

If Ruth hadn't taken the time to listen to Naomi's advice, she would
have missed out on marrying Boaz and being in the lineage of Jesus.

Ruth placed herself in a position to be mentored, and by doing so, she chose to receive instruction from God through this older godly woman.

When we decide to take the time and effort to be mentored by a godly woman, we're doing much more than just soliciting someone else's opinion. We're inviting the instruction of the Holy Spirit to speak through her and show us the way to go. We're choosing to show humility, a teachable spirit, and a willingness to trust and share with the other person. When that happens, we in turn prepare to be the Holy Spirit's instrument to speak to those we mentor. Because mentoring requires commitment, it is often inconvenient, and it requires deliberate effort, wisdom, and time. So be wise about who and how many you commit to mentor.

God pours into us through someone, and we pour out to someone else. As we teach others, the truth is embedded more deeply in us. Our growth is stunted when we don't give.

Do you really have time *not* to mentor and be mentored?

✳

REBECCA ✳ One summer afternoon some time ago I was standing beside the small storage barn in my backyard, pouring out my heart to Evie on the other end of the phone line. She listened with a great deal of understanding as I shared with her my fears that I'd once again face burnout, and that I would someday hit the wall and be crippled by the crash. I'll never forget what she told me that day. She said, "Rebecca, just you being aware of this weakness will help you guard against it ever happening and will help bring victory over it."

Months later, a younger female friend for whom I've become an informal mentor shared her heart with me. She told of insecurities in her life that she feared would turn into actions and then into hardness of heart. I began to share with her, "My friend, just you being aware of this weakness will help you . . ."

I discovered afresh the joy and beauty of having—and being—a mentor. ✳

✳ **SHEism** ✳ A truly mentored SHE is a woman who understands and uses the powerful tool of mentoring to enrich both her own life and the life of others.

Additional Resources:

Bobb Biehl, Mentoring: **Confidence in Finding a Mentor and Becoming One** (Nashville: Broadman & Holman, 1996)

Gary Collins, **Christian Coaching: Helping Others Turn Potential into Reality** (Colorado Springs: NavPress, 2001)

Ted Engstrom, contributor, **The Fine Art of Mentoring: Passing On to Others What God Has Given to You** (Brentwood, Tenn.: Wolgemuth and Hyatt, 1989)

Howard G. Hendricks, **As Iron Sharpens Iron: Building Character in a Mentoring Relationship** (Chicago: Moody Press, 1995)

Betty Huizenga, **Gifts of Gold: Gathering, Training, and Encouraging Mentors** (Colorado Springs: David C. Cook Publishing, 2002)

"To have the greatest serenity and influence as Christians, we must live within God's boundaries, because it is there, embraced by his love and protected by his grace, that we enjoy the sweetest liberty."

Barbara Johnson *The Women of Faith Devotional*[1]

> "The boundary lines have fallen for me in pleasant places."

Psalm 16:6, NIV

Chapter 9

Boundaried: Building Life-Fences

❋ Kay allows her monthly cycle to affect her emotional responses.

❋ Ann takes care of everyone in her family except herself.

❋ Carmen is influenced by all kinds of "spiritual-improvement" fads.

❋ Donna goes from one bad relationship to another.

❋ Susan's spending is out of control.

❋ Tonya's life is so disorganized, she doesn't know how to regain control.

What do all these women have in common? They lack boundaries. Though many people today struggle in this area, some are wising up to the reality of our seemingly epidemic lack of balance. According to a *USA Today* article, the town of Ridgewood, New Jersey, set out to redefine some much-needed guidelines. They determined to draw boundaries—if only temporary ones—around the overstretched schedules of their citizens. Here's how the article described this reclaiming effort:

> No homework, no practice, no clarinet lessons.
> No math league, no soccer, no SAT sessions.
> No swim meet, no Scout meet, no learning to sing.
> None of their usual scheduled things!

A committee of eighteen people spent seven months planning a night off for residents of the affluent East Coast town. The purpose of the Ridgewood Family Night was to allow families an evening to spend together—an evening of thoroughly unplanned time to slow down and enjoy each other.[2]

This night-off celebration was Ridgeway's answer to problems common in all of today's society. The "century two thousand" in which we now live might be renamed the "century 'too' thousand." We are too busy, too overworked, too overcommitted, too well fed, too entertained, too stressed, and as a result, too unhappy. We are a culture without boundaries—not just in the areas of time and commitment, but in most other areas, as well.

REBECCA ❋ During the writing of this book, I experienced a plane flight from Chicago to Nashville that twice affirmed the need for this chapter on boundaries. First, as I boarded my flight, I noticed a lady in front of me holding a book that offered hope and insights to people with an overloaded life. Then, minutes later, I sat down in my window seat and looked outside in anticipation of our takeoff. Suddenly I noticed a large fly trapped between the windowpanes. Lacking food and oxygen, I realized that little guy's chances of survival were slim—unless he found the way out through which he had come.

As I watched the insect stumble and fall as he searched for an exit, he reminded me of myself a few years ago. It was a time in my life when I was so boundary-less and overloaded that I cried daily. I could not see a way out of my exhaustion. One extra thing added to my already packed schedule would send me over the edge. Like the fly captured in the window, I realized that the key to getting out was to retrace my steps, exit where I had entered, then to say "no" one boundary at a time.

This chapter is about addressing our boundary problems and rediscovering balance in a world that seems to have lost the art. ✳

Forty years ago, scientist Dr. Hans Selye wrote about the excess stress we face as a result of our hectic lifestyle and the body's difficulty adjusting. He described two kinds of stress: Pleasant stress, which consists of enjoyable things that happen to us, such as Christmas and birthdays; and unpleasant stress, which might include the death of a loved one or a job change. We could compare the body to an eight-ounce glass being poured into by both good and bad stress pitchers. The glass still holds only eight ounces no matter whether the water flowing into it is pleasant or unpleasant. Overflow results.[3]

The complex schedules we face, combined with our inability to manage them through healthy boundaries, result in major stress overflow. Can you relate?

✳ Do you constantly run from one activity or commitment to another?

✳ Do you often feel emotionally unable to cope with the expectations placed on you at work and at home?

✳ Do you struggle with knowing where to draw the line for your own body in the areas of food, rest, exercise, or sex?

✳ Do you feel that you are lacking in the area of good time management?

✳ Have you overextended yourself financially?

✳ Do you have trouble recognizing the signs of spiritual abuse and manipulation?

✳ Do you often feel out of control?

If you answered yes to any of these questions and want things to change, read on. We don't intend to build your boundaries for you. Instead, we want to help you develop a time-proven template for drawing—or redrawing—healthy boundaries and for taking control of your life from this point forward.

Boundaries Defined

REBECCA ✳ I learned at an early age about the importance of boundaries. When I was about eight years old, my family and I stayed at my grandparents' house during the holidays. Of my six siblings, my brother Daniel is closest to my age. Probably because we were the older, more responsible children, we got lumped into a bed together. I had a feeling that wasn't going to work out from the get-go, so I warned him, "Stay on your side!" He must have seen this as an invitation to annoy me, because soon afterward, a foot crept over to my side of the bed and touched me on the leg. I, the ever-patient and mature older sister, kicked it back. The war continued until a higher authority in the form of our mother entered the room and the blame games began. Soon enough, the boundary lines were drawn by a rolled-up blanket down the middle of the bed. ✳

Psychologists and boundary experts Drs. Henry Cloud and John Townsend acknowledge our need for boundaries from childhood to old age. The first of their books on this subject, appropriately called *Boundaries,* sold more than one million copies. Subsequent successful boundary books followed for kids, couples, marriages—everything but pets. Cloud and Townsend write, "Boundaries define us. They define what is me and what is not me. A boundary shows me where I end and someone else begins, leading me to a sense of ownership."[4]

Author Randy Alcorn writes about a person's need for godly boundaries:

> *A smart traveler doesn't curse guardrails. He doesn't whine, "The guardrails dented my fender!" He looks over the cliff, sees demolished autos, and thanks God for guardrails. God's guardrails*

are His moral laws. They stand between us and destruction. They are there not to punish or deprive us, but to protect us.[5]

In this chapter, we would like to describe a boundary as a "life-fence." A fence is built to mark property lines, so you know what belongs to you and what belongs to your neighbor. As Ridgeway, New Jersey, discovered, drawing boundaries involves what we will and won't do. However, boundaries—or life- fences—are effective only when they're consistently enforced to define our way of life.

Some of you may think you don't need to worry about life-fences. Early American colonists didn't think they needed fences either. At first, wide-open, unrestrained spaces seemed to provide endless opportunities and freedom, but it didn't take long for settlers to learn that they needed fences for protection and to acquire a sense of ownership of their land. It was not until their fences were built that they found true freedom and peace of mind.

From the earliest enclosures to invisible fencing of today, fences have provided much-needed boundaries for keeping the good in and the bad out. Whether they're for identifying personal property or protecting us from danger, we also need to build life-fences.

Boundaries Times Six

As children learning to color, many of us were taught to outline the pictures with crayons before filling them in. Doing so helped us stay in the lines. Unfortunately, as we grow and put away our crayons, we often forget to continue to outline our personal and relational boundaries and work safely within them. As a result, our life is not clearly defined, and it becomes subjected to circumstances and the whims of others. This lack of guidelines in governing ourselves becomes evident in both our actions and in the actions we accept from others. Though many boundary areas exist, the most common six might be the following:

Emotional Boundaries

You worry about the future. Anger overtakes your reason. You allow unhealthy people to influence you.

Emotional boundaries provide needed guidelines for how we

respond to our feelings. They involve both the way we handle our emotions and the degree to which we allow ourselves to be affected by others.

LYNDA ✳ Not too long ago my husband listened patiently as I cried and spoke passionately about something he had done that I didn't like. I was sure Dave needed to know how I felt. After all, it had been all I could think about for several hours. The more I dwelt on the issues, the bigger they got, so I let him have it. Tears flowed as I spilled out my feelings. Dave listened calmly as he always does, which fueled my emotions even more. Once I had said all I could think of, I left and went to the bathroom to wash my face. Boy did I need makeup!

I kept a cold distance from him for the rest of the day and that evening. Wouldn't you know it, the next morning I couldn't remember why I'd been so upset the day before. I recalled the issue but not the fervor. I let it percolate a little while, and then I went to Dave again. Based on his experience the day before, he probably dreaded what would come next. But then I said, "Remember what we—okay I— talked about yesterday? Well, it still matters to me today, but only about 20 percent of the amount it mattered yesterday. I still mean what I said, but not as much as I did then." ✳

Drawing emotional boundaries does not mean we stifle how we feel. Instead, we learn to understand and manage our emotions, while at the same time keeping a healthy distance from the uncontrolled, unreliable emotions of others. As women, we understand that emotions are a bigger factor for us than they are for men, and they grow more intense some times of the month than others. It must have been part of God's curse for women after Eve's first sin (as was the growth of nose hair in men!).

Physical Boundaries

You overextend yourself for everyone else. You struggle with sexual boundaries. You misuse your body.

Physical boundaries make the rules for how we take care of our body. They also request that others honor our rules too. When physical boundaries are not enforced, we neglect the things that are good for us and allow harmful things instead. We eat too much, exercise too infrequently, and rest too little, or we give in to sexual pressure because of weak moral fences. Guilt inevitably follows, which chips away at our self-esteem, which then invites poor, disrespectful treatment from others.

> When physical boundaries are not enforced, we neglect the things that are good for us and allow harmful things instead.

Spiritual Boundaries

Your interest in spiritual matters runs hot and cold. You're unable to recognize wrong spiritual teaching or leadership. You depend on others for your spiritual growth. You don't prioritize your personal relationship with God.

Spiritual boundaries are constructed from the bricks of God's Word, which tell us how to grow closer to Him. They show us how to build our life based on His standards, not our own. But because we've maxed out the twenty-four hours we get each day, we don't *have* the time or *take* the time to consult these instructions or learn the biblical guidelines. Sometimes we read them but don't understand, so we stop spending time in these truths and depend on others—books, pastors, or radio Bible teachers—to feed us spiritual food. As a result, we find ourselves snacking on Sundays instead partaking in a daily diet of God's Word. This makes us unable to know good from bad teaching or right from wrong decisions. And we stop growing spiritually.

Relational Boundaries

You haven't developed empowering, fulfilling relationships with key people in your life. You choose unsafe people to date or befriend. You allow others to take advantage of you. You have codependent relationships.

Relational boundaries set guidelines for what we will and will not accept from others. Without them, we permit dangerous people to come near. We let others take advantage of us, and we don't develop lasting relationships.

Financial Boundaries

You feel discontented with the things you own. You live above your means. You abuse your credit. You hold on to your money so tightly that it has a hold over you.

Financial boundaries set up standards for how we will and will not spend the money we make. The areas of life on which we spend the most time and money reflect what's truly important to us. Before you read any further, take out your check registry and your most recent credit-card statement. Make a list of the things you bought. What did you discover?

Author of *The Cheapskate Monthly*, Mary Hunt found herself $100,000 in credit-card debt before she decided she desperately needed to build boundaries into her finances. These new life-fences ultimately took her to a zero balance, but in the process she learned much about herself and the reasons she got to that point in the first place. The late Larry Burkett, president of Crown Financial Ministries, often said during his radio broadcast that the way we spend our money is an outward indicator of our spiritual health.

Organizational Boundaries

You often feel overwhelmed by your schedule. Your home, mind, and life in general are disorganized. You consistently run late.

Organizational boundaries bring order to chaos. They find appropriate spots for everything—either by throwing away, giving away, or putting away. When we don't have organizational boundaries, clutter results. Clutter may come in the form of too many commitments, a disorganized and frantic mind, or a lack of order in your home. When these and other areas aren't in appropriate balance, chaos results.

Which life-fences do you need to build? Emotional? Physical? Spiritual? Relational? Financial? Organizational? Maybe several—or maybe all of these. The first step in strengthening life-fences is recognizing the need for them; the second step is recognizing what it takes to build them.

Drawing Up the Plans

LYNDA ✴ When I was a child, my dad decided we needed a new garage. After his decision was made, Dad's next step was to tally the cost and gather the materials for the job.

The same is true for constructing your life-fences. You've realized you need to build, reinforce, or restructure at least one fence in your life. Now it's time to determine the cost and what it will take to get it done: ✳

What's the purpose of your boundary?

Just as a fence can serve as protection, containment, or the demarcation of what is legally yours, life-fences serve various purposes too. Maybe you need a boundary to decide, define, and describe who you are and what your part will and will not be in one of the six areas mentioned above. Perhaps it's time to protect yourself. Just plain privacy might be your motivation for building life-fences into your world.

All life-fences, regardless of their function, have some things in common:

✳ They bring peace and security to their owner.

✳ They provide confidence in moving forward.

✳ They create consistency for our decisions.

✳ They can please God.

✳ They bring balance.

Who's affected by your boundaries?

Before you build a fence around a yard, you need to consult everyone, including neighbors, who will be affected by its construction. The cliché "Good fences make good neighbors" is true when those fences are understood beforehand.

Your life-fences need that too. Who are your stakeholders—those who will be impacted by your new boundaries? Extended family? Friends? Husband? Children? Coworkers? They need to hear from you, "From now on, things are going to be different." "Just because I'm single doesn't mean I should be taken advantage of." "I am married, and my first loyalty is to my husband. I won't let you interfere anymore!"

How do you build your boundaries?

> **LYNDA** ✳ A friend of mine I'll call Sue was dating Dan. They were sexually active. Then Sue became a Christian and learned about God's rules on purity. Though Dan hadn't yet followed her spiritual lead, Sue set forth new guidelines for their time alone to keep them from having sex until after they married. The new rules worked for the next two years until they said their vows, but not without Sue drawing a firm line. ✳

Informing your stakeholders of the difference your life-fences will bring will put them on alert. They'll be watching, however, to see if you follow through and if things really do change. It will be up to you to draw boundaries within those boundaries—specific ideas for carrying them out. You should tell your stakeholders not only about your decision to build new life-fences, but also what that will involve and specifically how it will affect each of them individually.

How do you decide what belongs inside and what stays outside?

A big part of being boundaried is prioritizing those you let inside your fences, those for whom you let your "de-fences" down. You are in control of your gate. You're the one who decides who and what belong inside and outside your life-fence. You're the one who makes—and enforces—the rules of entrance.

In another of their books, Cloud and Townsend point out ways to recognize unsafe people:[6]

Personal Traits

✳ appear to have it all together

✳ are religious, not spiritual

✳ are defensive

✳ are self-righteous

✳ don't apologize

✳ avoid working on problems

❊ demand trust

❊ claim they are perfect

❊ blame others for problems

❊ lie and deceive

❊ are stagnant

Interpersonal Traits
❊ avoid closeness

❊ are only concerned about themselves

❊ resist freedom of others

❊ flatter us

❊ are condemning

❊ relate as parent/child

❊ are unstable over time

❊ are a negative influence

You can decide who the safe people are by making a list of qualities opposite of the ones listed above. The list might include descriptions like:

❊ honest

❊ spiritually sound

❊ humble

❊ apologetic when necessary

❊ effective problem solvers

❊ trustworthy

* willing to accept responsibility for their actions

* growing

. . . and the "safe" list goes on.

We need to remember one thing, however. While we shouldn't spend the majority of our time in the company of unsafe people, sometimes God calls us to reach out to them for the purpose of promoting healing in their life.

How do you maintain your boundaries?

LYNDA * I once knew a woman I'll call Nancy, whose husband misused the Bible's definition of submission and demanded that she comply to his demands "because God says so!" Nancy finally saw a Christian counselor, who showed her how to set healthy boundaries. Nancy still sees herself as a submissive wife, but not in the way she once did. She now considers her husband's requests and asks herself, *Will this hurt me in any way?* If the answer is yes, she quickly draws the line. After a while, her husband learned he couldn't get away with bullying Nancy any longer. *

A fence is only as effective as its weakest link. Intruders can find their way through broken places. It will be up to you to quickly make repairs once breaks happen either over time or because of deliberate attacks.

Two actions will be involved on your part in order to keep your life-fences strong: maintenance and repair. You will need to inspect your boundaries often to discover possible wear and tear. Sometimes you will need to reestablish boundaries that were built long ago but have been neglected over time. Examples might include rebuilding self-protective ways of dealing with a friend who betrays your confidence, a boyfriend who tries to take physical liberties, or an overwhelming schedule that leaves you feeling like you're dying inside. Stand close to your life-fences in order to guard them. The quicker you yell at a stray dog who wanders into your yard, the quicker he'll think twice about whether or not he'll return.

Bookstores and libraries are full of books that explain how to build fences from beginning to end. No one sets out on a construction project without a set of plans to show how to proceed.

You'll need to do the same in your personal life. You'll need to consult the Manual to show you how to plan, build, maintain, and repair effective life-fences. That manual is the Bible.

Who Am I? (Proverbs 8:22-34)

I know about building boundaries. I am the very first SHE. Do you know who I am?

Some of you probably answered Eve or Mary of Nazareth, but no; I existed long before they did. I'll give you a hint from a book that tells my story:

> *The Lord formed me from the beginning, before he created anything else. I was appointed in ages past, at the very first, before the earth began. I was born before the oceans were created, before the springs bubbled forth their waters . . . before the mountains and the hills were formed . . . before he had made the earth and fields and the first handfuls of soil.*[7]

I was born even before God created the world you live in:

> *I was there when he established the heavens, when he drew the horizon on the oceans . . . when he set the clouds above, when he established the deep fountains of the earth . . . when he set the limits of the seas, so they would not spread beyond their boundaries . . . when he marked off the earth's foundations.*[8]

I was there to help God draw the boundaries for everything that would be, for everything that would come:

> *I was the architect at his side. I was his constant delight, rejoicing always in his presence.*[9]

My name is Wisdom, and I am SHE. I existed then to help God draw the boundaries of the earth, and I exist now to help you draw the boundaries for your life:

And so, my children, listen to me, for happy are all who follow my ways. Listen to my counsel and be wise. Don't ignore it. Happy are those who listen to me.[10]

Today, I extend my hand and invite you to walk alongside me for the rest of your life. I would love to be your architect, your constant delight, as I was with God. Let me show you how to make every decision, every day, from this point forward. Let me show you how to build and maintain your life-fences. Think of the most beautiful place you have ever seen. We—God and I—drew those boundaries! Don't you think I can show you how to draw your boundaries too?

I am Wisdom. I impart my instruction to you today through the Bible, God's Word. Since healthy boundaries are based on me, Wisdom, when you face a decision, just ask yourself, *Is it wise?* Then go to the Word. I'm waiting to show you your answer. "For whoever finds me finds life and wins approval from the Lord."[12]

Boundaries and You

Wisdom's middle name is Truth, so to speak. Everything she advises is based on principles that will never change or let you down. Everything Wisdom opposes revolves around a lie that will ultimately hurt you. Choose the truth over the lie. Choose Wisdom!

·· ✳ *SHE Lives the Truth* ✳ ··

1. When I turn everything over to God, through Him I gain control of my emotions.

Lie: My emotions are uncontrollable!

LYNDA ✳ Earlier in this chapter I described my emotional confrontation with Dave. I also told you about my coming-to-my-senses experience the next day. I've talked long and hard with God about giving me emotional balance. I feel like one of the morsels of wisdom He's given me is this: *Wait to respond, and if it still matters later, take it to the next step.* Dave would tell you I'm far from perfect, but he knows I've decided to let Wisdom show me how to control my emotions and not live my life allowing them to control me. ✳

Whether it's worry, anger, hurt, or bitterness, Wisdom tells us not to let it take root in us.

> **REBECCA** ✳ In *Wait for Me*, I tell a story about something a counselor friend of mine from Australia told me that has helped me to let go of worrisome fears: "If you let the bird of unhealthy nonreality-based fears nest or roost in your mind, it can wreak all kinds of havoc. Instead, what we must do with these fears is not let them roost, but fly overhead—over top of us."[13] ✳

In addition to controlling our emotions, Wisdom tells us to protect them.

> **LYNDA** ✳ My mother says there's a rose inside each of us that can be battered only so many times before it dies. Guard your emotions at all costs! Watch out for the circumstances you've exposed them to and ask, *Is it wise?* ✳

The Bible not only acknowledges the fact that we have emotions, but it shows what we can do to control and protect them in godly ways. This allows us to stay confidently inside our emotional life-fences, which God's Wisdom has helped us build.

WORDS TO THE WISE:

Proverbs 4:23: *Above all else, guard your heart, for it affects everything you do.*

Ephesians 4:26: *Don't sin by letting anger gain control over you.*

Proverbs 21:19: *It is better to live alone in the desert than with a crabby, complaining wife.*

2. When I hurt myself by not living with physical boundaries, I hurt others too.

Lie: *I'm a grown adult and can do as I please with my body as long as I'm not hurting anyone.*

If we don't rest up, we can't give effectively, and we, along with everyone around us, pay for it.

REBECCA ✳ My mum has often reminded me of the importance of taking care of ourselves so we can properly take care of others. Though I'm not married and do not have children, ministry feels like a child at times with its demands and expectations, so I learned this lesson early. ✳

Whether taking care of yourself means napping or saying no to unnecessary obligations, we must take in so we can give out. That includes eating, exercising, and resting right. Some of us need much sleep, others less. Some enjoy jogging, others swimming. Some require constant company; others need space. We know ourselves and what we need. It takes this kind of self-knowledge to build our physical life-fences as we learn to consistently ask ourselves, *Is it wise?*

The way we take care of our body is only one part of physical boundaries; what we require of others in relation to us is another.

REBECCA ✳ As a single woman, I have upheld strict dating life-fences. For example, I maintain a "shoe in the door" policy with guys I date. If circumstances are such that we happen to be in a room alone together, especially at night, I literally put a shoe in the door to prop it open. This way we both know that someone could walk in at any moment. Though taking this stand hasn't been easy at times, it has helped me in my effort to live above reproach. Dating only Christian men and keeping accountable to people in my life are other biblical boundaries that I stick to without exception. I know that if I don't, my wrong choices will affect not only myself but everyone else in my life too. ✳

We need to develop "shoe in the gate" policies too, for letting people inside our boundaries and enforcing the rules for when they get there. How will you determine ahead of time what your physical boundaries will be? By deciding . . .

✳ "I will allow . . ."

✳ "I will not allow . . ."

Make these rules a regular part of your life, and keep people in your life to make sure you do.

WORDS TO THE WISE:

> 2 Corinthians 6:14, MSG: *Don't become partners with those who reject God.*

> 1 Corinthians 6:13-14, MSG: *You know the old saying, "First you eat to live, and then you live to eat"? Well, it may be true that the body is only a temporary thing, but that's no excuse for stuffing your body with food, or indulging it with sex. Since the Master honors you with a body, honor him with your body!*

> Proverbs 4:22: *[My words] bring life and radiant health to anyone who discovers their meaning.*

3. Spiritual boundaries give me timeless guidelines for right and wrong and keep me disciplined.

Lie: I have no need for spiritual boundaries.

REBECCA ✳ My friend Vanessa learned the hard way about her need for spiritual boundaries. Here's how she described her experience after she asked herself, *Is it wise?*

> *The pastor [of my former church] was trying to put himself in the place of God. He was saying that we don't hear from God as well as he does, and that is why he said that we always need to ask for his permission before we do anything. . . . I knew that I needed to leave when the pastor told me that he is never wrong.* ✳

Like Vanessa, we need to know the Word ourselves so we can judge what is truth and what is spiritual manipulation. We need to keep:

Within Our Life-Fence	Outside Our Life-Fence
Teaching that agrees with the Bible	Teaching that contradicts the Bible
Right living	Lifestyles God says are wrong
Biblical wisdom	Worldly wisdom

Another important aspect of building and maintaining spiritual boundaries is protecting your relationship with God. In a world that is constantly trying to steal your time, affection, and focus, you must be committed to keeping your time with God inside your boundaries and distractions outside.

Build every section of your life-fence based on the Bible. Also, consult other godly people whose opinions you trust and whose own spiritual guidelines are evident.

WORDS TO THE WISE:

Proverbs 21:21: *Whoever pursues godliness and unfailing love will find life, godliness, and honor.*

Proverbs 15:22: *Plans go wrong for lack of advice; many counselors bring success.*

4. God made me to need people, and I need Him to show me how to develop healthy relationships and prioritize them properly.

Lie: I don't need relational boundaries. I can say yes to everyone and all their requests.

REBECCA ❊ I have seen a disturbing problem in the life of many women my mum's age. It has to do with the empty-nest syndrome. It's been said that many women get much of their self-esteem from their children while men often get their sense of self-worth from their job. A problem arises when the children leave and the marriage has been neglected because of wrongly placed priorities. Many couples find when their children leave they no longer know each other. ❊

A godly way of prioritizing relationships looks like this for the married woman: (1) God; (2) spouse; (3) children; (4) job, ministry, etc. The single woman's priority list looks like this: (1) God; (2) family and friends; (3) job, ministry, etc. Every one of our boundary problems can be traced back to some kind of misplaced priority. If we say yes to everything, we're not giving priority to the most important things.

So before you give much attention to something or someone in your life, ask yourself, *Is it a priority? Is it wise?*

WORDS TO THE WISE:

Proverbs 8:12, 14: *I, Wisdom, live together with good judgment. I know where to discover knowledge and discernment. . . . Good advice and success belong to me. Insight and strength are mine.*

Proverbs 13:20: *Whoever walks with the wise will become wise; whoever walks with fools will suffer harm.*

5. I spend, I pay.

Lie: I can have anything I want. I don't have to think about the cost right now.

LYNDA ✳ When my daughter Courtney was in her midteens and making some babysitting money, we helped her open a checking account. Time went by, and Courtney began to talk about how God was blessing her. "Every time I pay my tithes, I get another babysitting job. It seems like God is multiplying the money I have."

It did seem as though spiritual multiplication was taking place—until we received a statement from the bank. We had failed to tell Courtney that a $1,000 reserve line had been attached to protect her from overdrafts. She had been spending without planning or keeping track, and it had finally caught up to her. It was time to pay the piper! ✳

Many of us as adults think along the same lines young Courtney did. We act as though we can keep spending the money, and it will keep being there. The fact is, if it hasn't already happened it will happen one day: Your piper bill will come due.

God does bless His people, but He first requires that we follow His ways. Those ways include the need to tithe, to be content and thankful, and to be wise. Before you spend, give your decision some time. Don't buy that dress today. Go home and look in your checkbook. Examine your closet for what you already have. Then ask yourself, *Is it wise?*

If you draw those life-fences around your money decisions, things will turn around for you financially.

WORDS TO THE WISE:

Proverbs 10:16: *The earnings of the godly enhance their lives, but evil people squander their money on sin.*

Proverbs 13:11: *Wealth from get-rich-quick schemes quickly disappears; wealth from hard work grows.*

6. My life is short, and I'm to live it effectively, not in peace-stealing disarray.

Lie: Organization is overrated.

REBECCA ✳ My best friend, Karleen, is twenty-six and the homeschooling mother of three girls under the age of six. Her job can be rather overwhelming at times, but she has come to realize that the tidiness of her house affects her attitude. So Karleen builds into her schedule a time to clean and organize. By doing so, she is succeeding in her more important jobs, such as spending quality time with her kids, without feeling overwhelmed and imbalanced. ✳

LYNDA ✳ I need to always have my house straight on the surface before I work well. Take a look in my purse, closets, and dresser drawers, however, and you'll find a different story. What I find works best for me is not to list every one of my to-do jobs, but to add one straightening job to my normal routine every week, and I slowly get them caught up. ✳

Do one window a day, and you'll eventually be able to see the sunshine again. Build organizational life-fences, and you'll eventually be able to see the light of day.

WORDS TO THE WISE:

Proverbs 3:21-22: *My child, don't lose sight of good planning and insight. Hang on to them, for they fill you with life and bring you honor and respect.*

Psalm 90:12: *Teach us to make the most of our time, so that we may grow in wisdom.*

*

To be empowered women, we need boundaries, and to have proper boundaries, we need constant wisdom. The quicker we get wisdom, the quicker we'll establish needed boundaries. And the quicker we get boundaries, the sooner we'll become empowered.

LYNDA * I once set out to paper our basement family room. I decided I could hang straight pieces by just eyeballing the wall and without the benefit of a plumb line. So I hung the first piece, and the second, and it was looking pretty good—good, that is, until I arrived at the end. When the last piece met the first piece, I cringed as I saw the six-inch difference between the top and bottom of the strip of paper. My problem could've been avoided if I'd bothered to use the plumb line from the beginning. *

If you've hung some wrong pieces of your life without using the plumb line of Wisdom, start again. Teach others you know the importance of seeking Wisdom. Ask yourself and teach them to ask, *Is it wise?*

May God be with you every moment from this point forward, as you allow Wisdom to show you how to plan, build, guard, maintain, and repair your life-fences and help others do the same. Wisdom is a terrible thing to waste.

Don't turn your back on wisdom, for she will protect you. Love her, and she will guard you. . . . If you prize wisdom, she will exalt you. Embrace her and she will honor you.

Proverbs 4:6, 8

✳ **SHEism** ✳ The truly boundaried SHE is a woman who asks herself, *Is it wise?* and becomes empowered by building and maintaining strong, biblical life-fences.

Additional Resources:

Henry Cloud and John Townsend, **Boundaries** (Grand Rapids, Mich.: Zondervan, 1992)

Richard A. Swenson, **Margin: How to Create the Emotional, Physical, Financial, and Time Reserves You Need** (Colorado Springs,: NavPress, 1992)

"If we truly desire to know our destiny, the purpose for which we were created, there is only one place to turn in our search—to the Creator, the Author of meaning and purpose."

Kathy Peel *Discover Your Destiny*[1]

Chapter 10

Purposeful: More than Drifting

So far in our journey to SHEdom, we've discussed how to be safe—protected, intimate, and feminine—God's way. We've discovered the biblical path to becoming healthy—beautiful, pure, and free. Now, before we leave the subject of empowerment, we'd be remiss if we didn't also address how to become purposeful. Purpose will take you to the next level. It will provide strength, direction, and focus for where you go from here. And purpose will give you enthusiasm about today as well as hope for tomorrow.

An article that appeared in *Financial Times* illustrates the deathly response of many in the absence of the hope that purpose provides:

> *In recent decades, Japan's punctual railways have symbolized the efficiency and power of Japan's economy. Now they are highlighting another trend—the social cost of the downturn.*

Faced with a rise in the number of people throwing themselves under trains, East Japan Railway, the busiest carrier in the world, has come up with an unusual response.

The company plans to place mirrors on the tracks and paint its railway crossings in dazzling colors to deter would-be suicide victims from jumping.[2]

How have we allowed the reason for our existence to be reduced to the job we hold, the things we possess, or the title we carry? When did we relinquish control of our hope and empowerment to a slight change in our circumstances? And what kind of day and age do we live in when a railway company has to put mirrors on the tracks to attempt to stop an epidemic number of suicides? A day and age that is largely devoid of purpose.

✳ What about you?

✳ Do you feel confused about your purpose in life?

✳ Do you have a God-given vision for the future?

✳ Do you feel that you are on a daily mission?

Purposeless or PurposeFULL?

In Lewis Carroll's classic children's tale *Alice's Adventures in Wonderland,* Alice comes to a fork in the road. She asks the Cheshire Cat which direction she should take. The Cat responds that it depends a great deal on where she'd like to go, to which Alice replies that she doesn't care much. "Then it doesn't matter which way you walk," the Cat answers.

You and I face similar choices and forks in the road each day. If we, like Alice, don't care where we are headed, then we will probably find ourselves in a spiritual no-man's-land. But if we are seeking to live an impactful life, with our steps ordered by God, then our direction matters greatly. So how can we determine which road we should take?

By discovering and living out our God-given purpose.

Since the beginning, everything God has done has been on purpose.[3] He not only created things by speaking them into being, He also gave each creation a purpose. The sky separates the water above from the water beneath. Land produces vegetation and living creatures. Lights separates day from night[4]:

> For everything, absolutely everything, above and below, visible and invisible . . . everything got started in him and finds its purpose in him.[5]

Since God built purpose into everything else He made, it's no surprise that He designed us for a purpose too. One of the most powerful cravings of the human spirit is to find a sense of significance and relevance, an individual reason for existence. Purpose is the key to life. Without it, life has no meaning.

It would seem that Christians should have a better idea of why God created us. In reality, however, many of us feel as aimless as Alice. We see finding God's will and purpose for our life like chasing the elusive pot of gold at the end of the rainbow. Look *around* you. Look *at* you. How are you seeing life lived out by others? We talked in chapter 2 about Abraham Maslow's hierarchy of needs: fundamental needs (safety, food, and water), psychological needs (belonging, acceptance, and competence), self-actualization needs (fulfilling unique potential).

We called these s*afe, healthy,* and e*mpowered.* We could also name them: survival mode, success mode, significance mode.

In which mode do you spend most of your life?

If you're living in *survival mode,* you're just maintaining, merely surviving, even if you know Christ. Your life consists of just another day of robotically working, sleeping, working, sleeping. You're merely getting by, and you find yourself living for that two weeks of vacation or that perfect man to sweep you off your feet or that ideal job to fulfill you and pay what you're worth. What you find, however, is that none of these things ever measures up to what you needed *or* expected.

In *success mode,* you put all your eggs in one basket with a label marked "Success." You stay busy trying to make something of yourself—trying to earn, achieve, and qualify. You equate success with accomplishment. You measure your achievements by what others say and expect of you, things you accumulate, and recognition you receive. Yet inside you feel empty, unfulfilled, and purposeless. Poet Edwin Arlington Robinson wrote his classic poem "Richard Cory" about someone whose success-mode living brought meaningless desperation:

> *Whenever Richard Cory went down town,*
> *We people on the pavement looked at him:*
> *He was a gentleman from sole to crown,*
> *Clean favored and imperially slim.*
>
> *And he was always quietly arrayed,*
> *And he was always human when he talked;*
> *But still he fluttered pulses when he said,*
> *"Good–morning," and he glittered when he walked.*
>
> *And he was rich—yes, richer than a king,*
> *And admirably schooled in every grace:*
> *In fine—we thought that he was everything*
> *To make us wish that we were in his place.*
>
> *So on we worked, and waited for the light,*
> *And went without the meat, and cursed the bread;*
> *And Richard Cory, one calm summer night,*
> *Went home and put a bullet through his head.*

One of life's greatest tragedies is not death, but life without discovering individual God-given purpose. You don't really live unless you know why you're alive. Abundant life, as we defined in chapter 1, cannot be found in the survival or success mode. Consider the significance mode instead.

> One of life's greatest tragedies is not death, but life without discovering individual God-given purpose.

The Significance—or PurposeFULL— Mode

REBECCA ※ When I was twelve years old I attended a service at my Christian school that would significantly impact my life story. A speaker asked people to come forward if they felt God leading them to give their gifts and talents to Him. I felt led by God to respond and ask for His direction in discovering His will and purpose for my life. It was that same year that God began to lead me into music. ✳

LYNDA ✳ I had been teaching for four years. I liked my work, but I didn't love it, and I felt something calling me on to other things. So I began my search. I wasn't content to stay working in the same place for twenty years, and new experiences beckoned me. Thinking I had found my answer, I resigned from teaching and accepted a position in the business sector as a program coordinator. I hadn't been there long when I found myself once again in survival mode like many others around me who, at best, hoped to work up to success mode in their place of employment. Most of them appeared to live for their two weeks of vacation time each year, and the more ambitious of them found satisfaction in the recognition they would receive from those working over them. So my hunt—and my job search—continued as I tried to find that place of significance where what I did would matter and live on. It wasn't until I got serious about my faith that I began to find the purpose I was searching for. Then I realized it was neither the place nor length of my employment that brought about significance, but whether or not I placed God in the center of my seeking. ✳

Life can be more than survival or living for mere temporal success. God created us to fulfill our unique potential. He also made us to desire and to strive after that potential. Our quest for significance could be measured by the recent huge success of Rick Warren's *The Purpose-Driven Life*. Warren describes the purposes the Bible reveals for every Christian. He says:

You were planned for God's pleasure.
You were formed for God's family.
You were created to become like Christ.
You were shaped for serving God.

But Warren adds another dimension, and that is the personal or individual purpose for which each of us was uniquely designed: You were made for a mission.[6]

LYNDA ✳ I am part of the Hunter clan. It's my family name. The purpose of that role includes things like living a godly life, treating people as Christ would, loving each other, and sharing our faith. But besides my identity as part of the Hunter family, I'm also Lynda. Uniquely designed and fearfully made.[7] ✳

In the same way, God desires that *all* the members of His family love Him and love our neighbors as ourselves. Then He wants us to:

Know Him in a personal and intimate way.

We talked about this divine desire in chapter 3. Before they sinned, Adam and Eve walked and talked with God in the Garden of Eden. God wants nothing less than that for us.

> *"For I know the plans I have for you," says the Lord. "They are plans for good and not for disaster, to give you a future and a hope. In those days when you pray, I will listen. If you look for me in earnest, you will find me when you seek me."* [8]

Submit to His authority and let Him grow us into His image.

It began when He made us in His image:

> *God created people in his own image; God patterned them after himself; male and female he created them.* [9]

It continues and ends with God's desire that we grow to be like His Son.

> *For God knew his people in advance, and he chose them to become like his Son.* [10]

But God also plans that we individually . . .

Find and live out our unique purpose.

He wants us to be involved in His work.

> *God blessed them and told them, "Multiply and fill the earth and subdue it. Be masters over the fish and birds and all the animals."* [11]

The message is clear: To be human means that we have a purpose in life. We're here on a mission—both corporately and individually. We're here to recognize and be part of not only what God is doing in the whole world, but also what He wants to do individually through you and me. He wants us to find and fulfill our purpose.

And God is not hiding His purpose from us. In fact, He has the most to gain from our discovering our purpose and doing His will. As with everything we've talked about in this book, every aspect of becoming SHEs begins and ends with finding a personal relationship with our heavenly Father. If we haven't developed a friendship with God, His voice won't be familiar, and we won't be able to recognize it from the other voices in the world that are shouting at us. If you have accepted Christ's salvation, He *is* calling out His instructions and plans for you. You just need to listen, so you can both discover and live out your purpose in six key areas.

Purpose and the Six *P*'s

Our purpose doesn't exist in isolation. It also affects our potential, priorities, path, people, pitfalls, and peace. Let's see how.

1. Potential

> **LYNDA** ✳ Twenty-two-year-old Megan has been hurt by life, including by her mom and dad's divorce when she was three. As a result, she has grown to mistrust God. She doesn't think He has her best interest at heart because He allowed her family to fall apart, so she's afraid to turn her life over to Him. She told me she didn't want a faith like mine or anyone else's she knows. "That's because," I told her, "you are created for a different purpose. God has a plan for you that includes all your gifts and abilities, as well as your personality and interests. He wants you to have your own, unique relationship with Him." ✳

The same is true for all of us. God built into us the things we need—natural, inherent traits—for fulfilling His purpose. Our design is matched to the reason we exist, and that design predicts our potential. If we don't know our purpose, we probably will live beneath our potential.

In essence, we are the way we are because of *why* we are. God's assignments reveal our abilities and capabilities. Our potential is comprised of our unique gifts, abilities, and interests.

2. Priorities

Jesus first understood His purpose. Then He allowed that purpose to set His goals, which determined His decisions, predicted His choices, measured His progress, and set His priorities.

Since Jesus' purpose was to do His father's business, everything He spent His time on lined up with that purpose. His purpose defined His values. Those values determined what was right and what was wrong and what mattered and didn't matter to Him. Then He used those values to set His priorities.

> **LYNDA** ∗ When I worked as an elementary teacher, I had to create lesson plans for every class. Those plans required that I first establish a goal for each class time. Then I prioritized my time and wrote out specific objectives, all of which were directed at achieving my goal. Those objectives allowed me to see the end from the beginning. At any point throughout the lesson, I knew where I was headed. These plans and priorities allowed me to stay on track, and without them, the hour would have gone by without my getting any closer to the goal. ∗

Priorities protect us from being ineffective and giving too much attention to less important things. They help us choose the best stuff over the good stuff. They serve as guides for determining the right path, which will ultimately take us to the goal we've fixed our eyes upon. Then, like Jesus, we prioritize and make choices that keep us moving toward that goal. Life without specific, measurable objectives is vague and haphazard.

3. Path

In the 1950s, the U.S. Navy invented something called a Program Evaluation Review Technique (PERT). These PERTs were used to design a plan for certain projects they needed to accomplish. Simply put, they consisted of a beginning point, an ending point or goal, and the necessary steps needed on the path to accomplish that goal. They also included a time frame for each step. A PERT for cleaning the kitchen might look like this:

Messy Kitchen	Clearing Table	Loading Diswasher	Sweeping Floor	**Clean Kitchen**
	10 minutes	20 minutes	15 minutes	

We could view our lives as a series of PERTs too. The big PERT begins with our birth and ends when we die. In between, only you know the significant life experiences that affect your journey. Smaller PERTs, however, can help you reach productive intermittent goals. The process begins by looking at where you want to end up. Then you begin at the starting point—where you are today in regard to that goal—and decide what it will take to get there.

4. People

REBECCA ✳ Being a leader can be challenging at times. I have had to learn the hard way that you can't please everybody. Once when I was feeling weighed down by a coworker's not-so-happy response to my leadership decisions, God clearly spoke to me. I read in my Bible that I am called to serve the Lord with gladness.[12] In essence, I am to delight in fulfilling my purpose. I had allowed my concern about what others thought of me to steal my joy. Through this I came to understand that my main objective in life is to fulfill the calling God has given me and, while doing so, to be as loving as I can toward others. But I am not to be so people-pleasing that I become less God-pleasing. ✳

Though conflicts do arise as we seek to fulfill our purpose alongside others, fellowship with God-focused believers—most of the time, though not all of the time—can be empowering. Jesus hung out with like-minded people who shared His purpose. Abraham did too. The writer of Hebrews called Abraham's companions "fellow heirs with him of the same promise."[13] This time spent with fellow promise seekers helped prepare them for the work they were called to do. In his book *Renewing Your Spiritual Passion,* author Gordon Mac-Donald describes the types of people we associate with and what they can do to help or hinder our life's passion, which will in turn affect our purpose:

> Resourceful people *ignite* our passion.
> Important people [in our life] *share* our passion.
> Trainable people *catch* our passion.
> Nice people *enjoy* our passion.
> Draining people *sap* our passion.[14]

If we hang around with other purposeful people, they'll keep us moving toward our goal and focused and available for others who don't yet know why they were created.

5. Pitfalls

LYNDA ✳ I once heard a story of a man who traveled to India and watched workers weave beautiful Persian rugs. The workers were located in a circle around the master weaver, who sat in the center. The visitor asked one of the workers, "What do you do when you make a mistake? Throw it away? Start over?"

The worker answered, "We take what we've done to the master weaver. He carefully studies our work and mistakes, then he redesigns the total pattern so it incorporates the mistake we've made. Then we finish the work." ✳

God not only creates purpose, He recreates it too. If you're afraid your decisions have interfered with God's plan and purpose for your life, know that He has arranged a reformation program to redeem the detours. He's planned the total design so that it incorporates your wrong choices. God's purpose is not canceled because of your past. Purpose transforms mistakes into miracles and disappointments into testimonies.

> God's purpose is not canceled because of your past. Purpose transforms mistakes into miracles and disappointments into testimonies.

Gordon MacDonald goes on to describe some of the circumstances that destroy our passion and the pursuit of our purpose:

The drained condition:
depleted or exhausted energy or resources

The dried-out condition:
unchecked emotions, such as irritability and impatience

The distorted condition:
an obscured view of the way things really are, fed by the world's lies and inundating messages

The devastated condition:
fatigued and weary feelings that originate when people and events vigorously oppose what we stand for

The disillusioned condition:
deflated dreams

The defeated condition:
personal loss or defeat

The disheartened condition:
intimidated by people, events, or institutions that are seen as being more powerful than God[15]

Guard against circumstances and choices that thwart your pursuit of purpose. But if you do mess up, remember that your purpose remains, and God can help you get back on track.

6. Peace
When we feel like something is wrong about a decision we're making in search of our purpose, we sometimes say, "I just don't feel peace about it." We are alluding to the Holy Spirit speaking to a Christian and showing the way to go.

Psychologists call similar feelings *cognitive dissonance*, which is defined as "a tension that develops when someone holds two inconsistent thoughts at the same time."[16] Cognitive dissonance causes a sense of inner conflict or uncertainty. Relief comes only as we change either the way we feel or what we do about it. Experiencing a lack of peace (or cognitive dissonance) regarding a decision we're about to make could be coming from one of two sources: Either God is checking our spirit that we're making a wrong choice or Satan is attacking us to prevent the fulfillment of our purpose. Our job is to find out which it is. We can do this by talking to God.

* Ask Him to speak and to make His will clear to you.

* Ask Him to confirm His purpose through other means.

* Ask Him to not let you miss the right steps.

* Ask Him to give you peace.

Nothing can replace the peace that envelops us when we're smack dab in the center of God's will.

> Nothing can replace the peace that envelops us when we're smack dab in the center of God's will.

To live a purposeful life, you must move beyond the general mission for all Christians—to love God and glorify Him with your life—to the specific mission that is only yours. You won't live in a significant, purposeful, and empowered SHE mode until you do more than just live a lackluster life of survival or success. You'll know this is happening when you want more from your relationship with God. Nothing becomes dynamic until it becomes specific. Having a basic understanding of your life purpose is one thing; taking that purpose and investing in the journey to get there is another. Let's look at someone who has done it.

Esther: For Such a Time As This (Esther 1–10)

Queen Esther realized she was called to an individual purpose within a larger divine purpose. She was the wife of a Persian king named Xerxes, who ruled over 127 provinces from India to Ethiopia from 486 to 465 BC. Esther was not a Persian, but a Jewish orphan who had been raised by her cousin Mordecai, an exile from Jerusalem. He cared for her as a father, and she obeyed him like a daughter, even though she was the queen.

> To live a purposeful life, you must move beyond the general mission for all Christians—to love God and glorify Him with your life—to the specific mission that is only yours.

The king's ambitious chancellor, Haman, hated Jews. But the king respected him and commanded the people to bow down to him. When Mordecai refused to bow before anyone except God, Haman became enraged, and he built a gallows to kill Mordecai and determined to destroy all the other Jews in the Persian empire. The king had given Haman a type of power of attorney, which gave him the right to call the shots. Terror grew among the Jews.

At Mordecai's request, Esther had kept her Jewish heritage a secret from her husband and the people of the kingdom, but now Mordecai felt that the Jews would need Esther to intervene. "Go to your husband and ask for his help in saving your people," he said to Esther.

"Your people." That meant that Esther would have to reveal her Jewish heritage. How would the king react? Would he feel she had deceived him? Did he hate the Jews as much as Haman did?

Esther faced another obstacle too. No one was allowed to go before the king without being summoned—not even the queen. To do so would mean risking her life.

But Mordecai persisted. "Who knows whether you have come to the kingdom for such a time as this?" he said.[17]

Esther realized that if she remained silent, she might miss God's plan for her. God had not called for supernatural intervention to save His people. Angels had not been summoned to bombard the palace. The plan of escape God had designed for the Jews would be accomplished through one ordinary woman.

Esther called a three-day fast to seek God's guidance. Burning her bridges behind her, she determined to fulfill her purpose, even if it cost her life. She said, "If I perish, I perish."[18]

After days of prayer, Esther dressed in her best and walked into the presence of the king. She held her breath. Would she lose her life?

A hush fell over the room. Then slowly, ever so slowly, the king raised his golden scepter as proof that her life was safe. He asked, "What is your request, Queen Esther? It will be granted to you."

The first part of her prayer had been answered. Her life had been spared. But just as she recognized God had a plan for her, she also recognized He would accomplish it in His own time. Wisdom told Esther to delay making her urgent request, so she invited her husband and Haman to dinner. Again the king asked for Esther's request, but again she felt she should wait. "Come back tomorrow," she said.

That night when the king couldn't sleep, the courtier read to the king from the book of the chronicles, which recorded his reign. He listened to a story of how Mordecai had saved his life years earlier. King Xerxes decided it was time to honor Mordecai for his loyalty.

The next day at dinner, Esther knew it was time to make her request. She pleaded with the king to spare her people. Her words spoken the day before might have fallen on deaf ears. But Esther's devotion to her purpose and her wisdom in waiting had been aligned with God's divine timing and purpose.

Her husband responded, "Who was it who threatened the Jews?"

Esther pointed to Haman. "Then let him be hanged on the very gallows he built for Mordecai," the king commanded.

The course of history had been changed. Instead of killing the Jews, many people *converted* to the faith of the Jews by seeing the providence of their God.[19] The feast of Purim was instituted, in which even today, Jews all over the world celebrate what Queen Esther did for their people. Without her, the Jewish nation might have been annihilated. Jesus, the Messiah, was part of the Jewish nation. And without Him, the world would have been lost. But God used a woman He knew He could count on to fulfill her purpose, so His bigger purpose would also be fulfilled.

Purpose and You

Now it's time for you to focus in on your purpose—for such a time as this. Take out your journal or a clean sheet of paper and write your answers to these questions.

1. Everyone has talents, but God gives all His people—including me—special spiritual gifts to be used for His purpose.

Lie: I don't have any unique gifts or abilities.

❋ What has God uniquely gifted you to do?

❋ What do you do well?

❋ What are you interested in?

❋ What personality strengths and weaknesses do you observe in yourself? How do they affect your gifts?

TO MEMORIZE:

> Proverbs 18:16, NASB: *A man's gift makes room for him, and brings him before great men.*

> Romans 12:6: *God has given each of us the ability to do certain things well.*

2. I must learn to value and prioritize the things that will help me accomplish my purpose.

Lie: My life is so busy, I can't prioritize those things I value most.

❋ What are your goals? Short-term? Long-term?

❋ What are your values? your passions?

❋ If you knew tomorrow would be your last day on earth, how would you spend it?

❋ At the end of your life, what will you look back and say you accomplished?

❋ What adjectives would you say define your life?

✳ Is there a person or cause you're willing to die for?

✳ What single word would you want to be written on your tombstone?

✳ What important aspects of your life need to have higher priority and focus?

TO MEMORIZE:

> 1 Corinthians 6:12, NIV: *Everything is permissible for me—but not everything is beneficial.*

3. God designed me with a plan for my life.

Lie: My life has been so ordinary. God can't use a life as simple and plain as mine.

Brainstorm ten of the most significant events—both good and bad—that have happened in your life.

By looking back on these events, what pattern or plan can you see that led you in a certain direction?

Describe that direction. Draw your life PERT, which we described on pages 194–195, and the key events it includes.

Now draw a PERT that begins where you are right now and ends with the new, purposeful, changed you at the place you want to be. In the three steps, describe how you will move toward your new ending point.

Starting point:

> Step 1:
>
> Step 2:
>
> Step 3:
>
> *Ending point:*

TO MEMORIZE:

> Jeremiah 29:11, NIV: *"For I know the plans I have for you," declares the Lord, "plans to prosper you and not to harm you, plans to give you hope and a future."*

4. God has a whole world full of people with godly dreams that can link well with mine.

Lie: No one is going to support me in my unique purpose.

✳ Who are the five most purposeful people you know? What makes them so?

✳ What would you like to learn from them?

✳ Name five people you have spent an hour or more with in the past two weeks. Describe ways they either helped or hindered you in the pursuit of your purpose.

✳ Pray and look for people who will support you in your new sense of mission.

TO MEMORIZE:

Proverbs 27:9: *The heartfelt counsel of a friend is as sweet as perfume and incense.*

5. God not only created me for purpose, He recreates me for purpose too.

Lie: I've made so many mistakes, God can't possibly use me.

✳ What regrets do you have from your past?

✳ What choices have you made that you think messed up God's plans for your life?

✳ Do you believe that He can recreate you, mistakes and all, and use you for His good purpose?[20]

✳ How have you felt God's love, mercy, and forgiveness?

✳ What aspects of your lifestyle stand between you and God and the fulfillment of His plan for you? Any attitudes? emotions? motives? Write down these hindrances and ask God to forgive and recreate you. Then put them behind you. Today is a new day.

God never withdraws the gifts He gives, and He does not change His mind about those to whom He gives His grace or to whom He sends His call.

TO MEMORIZE:

> Romans 11:29, AMP: *For God's gifts and His call are irrevocable.*

6. God brings peace when I am right with Him and living out His purpose for my life.

Lie: I'll never find the peace of purposeful living.

✳ Do my actions reflect what I know to be right in the Bible and in my heart? Is this bringing me peace?

✳ How often do I feel truly peaceful?

✳ What do I do that brings the greatest peace?

✳ What people help support God's purpose and peace in my daily life?

✳ What tends to destroy my peace?

✳ What does my peace (or lack of peace) say about my life?

TO MEMORIZE:

> John 20:21: *[Jesus] spoke to them again and said, "Peace be with you. As the Father has sent me, so I send you."*

REBECCA: ✳ When I was fourteen, my family and I moved from Australia to the United States. My dad had accepted a job in Nashville, so my parents, my five brothers, and I began our American adventure. At the time, my parents thought they knew what God's purpose was in bringing us to a new country and a new life, but after a few months, we were unsure. My dad's promised job fell through, and we were left with no income, no furniture, no car, eight mouths to feed, and another baby on the way. During the coming months, we had to rely on God like never before. We prayed for our needs and saw checks unexpectedly arrive in the mail.

Doors opened for us to make money by cleaning houses, raking yards, and babysitting. Food and furniture appeared on our doorstep. One family gave us a minivan the same day they met us. I could write a whole book about all the miracles I watched God perform during that time.

Through the struggle and triumph of those times, God gave a fifteen-year-old girl a message to share that prayer is powerful and that God still does miracles when you trust Him. Now, more than a decade later, that grown-up girl travels around the world sharing about God's hope through music. My dad has a thriving Christian management company, and my three eldest brothers are serving God in their respective ministries.

Our family came to America knowing that God had called us here, but God had a greater purpose for us than we could have dreamed. ✳

✳

God has a greater purpose for you, too—more than you could ever dream. Be intentional about your purpose by writing out your life mission statement. Keep it in view, and seek to live it every day in every way. If you encounter distractions that are not in keeping with your mission, let them go. Pursue, instead, those things that line up with your life purpose. Doing so will allow you to accomplish the goals God gave you. In the process, you will find new meaning and empowerment for living. Go ahead. Live your life—on purpose.

✳ **SHEism** ✳ The truly purposeful SHE understands her unique calling and uses her abilities and gifts effectively for the glory of God.

Additional Resources:

Rick Warren, **The Purpose-Driven Life** (Grand Rapids, Mich.: Zondervan, 2002)

Bill Peel and Kathy Peel, **Discover Your Destiny** (Colorado Springs: NavPress, 1996)

Jan Johnson, **Living a Purpose-Full Life** (Colorado Springs: Waterbrook Press, 1999)

James Emery White, **You Can Experience a Purposeful Life** (Nashville: Word Publishing, 2000)

"The first thing which they realized up there on the slopes of the Kingdom of Love was how much more there would be to see and learn and understand when the King took them higher on future occasions."

Hannah Hurnard *Hinds' Feet on High Places*[1]

"No eye has seen, no ear has heard, no mind has conceived what God has prepared for those who love him."

1 Corinthians 2:9, NIV

Chapter 11

U R SHE

LYNDA ✳ I'll never forget the year I took my place on the living-room couch with my siblings as Dad sat in front of the Christmas tree on our turquoise, linoleum floor. One by one he picked up each gift, read the name, and passed it to its recipient. My familiar Christmas morning excitement jitters had arrived, though I knew Dad's small salary didn't go far in our large family. I was number two of what would be eight children born to our family over eighteen years. We each expected only a couple of gifts every season, but we appreciated them as much as our friends who received much more. Even the way we got our "free" Christmas trees in the university town we lived in had become a tradition. When the college quarters ended in early December, students would place their trees on the street outside their dorm for "townies" like us to pick up. Often, the one we selected was way too big for our living room. It bent slightly under the ceiling and spread throughout much of the room.

This mix of memories and tradition, as well as excitement and anticipation, overwhelmed me as Dad continued to read and pass that day. Squeals of delight sounded from my younger brothers and sisters as they opened their gifts. Eventually, the boxes wrapped in festive colors disappeared from under the tree, but I was left empty-handed. I didn't say anything, but my lip began to stiffen. By the time Dad had given out the final present, I had to fight back tears from all kinds of emotions—self-pity, hurt, and disappointment, as well as feelings of *Oh, it really doesn't matter anyway.*

Then Mom spoke: "Oops, I forgot one." She hurried out of the room and quickly returned carrying a small—and I mean small—box. She laid it in the palm of my hand. I remember thinking, *What, that's all? This is what I've been waiting for?*

I pulled back the wrapping, lifted the lid, and blinked my moist eyes as the sun reflected off the contents of my present—a silver charm bracelet. I had wanted one for a long time, and somewhere in my mind as I hugged and thanked my dad and mom, I realized that it had cost more than they had to spend. But in the years to follow, more charms symbolized significant events in my life, such as my sweet-sixteen birthday and my high-school graduation.

Recently I found that bracelet, now nearly forty years old. Tarnished with age, the chain slid between my fingers. Each charm brought back memories of the event it represented, though some were more special to me than others. Empty links showed where charms that hadn't been properly secured had been lost.

As I returned the bracelet to its box, even the memory of my disappointment at its size came back to me. The contents of bigger boxes I would receive through the years to come didn't leave lasting impressions. I can't really remember even one.

Then I realized that I had underestimated the bracelet's value because it was contained in such a little, unexpected place. What had seemed like just another Christmas morning became one I will never forget, as I discovered a very big gift in a very small package. ❊

Our Gift to You

When you opened this book, perhaps you thought it was just another read. Maybe you came upon it by accident and thought it would be no huge deal. But we hope that in years to come you'll see it as a big gift found in an unexpected place. We hope our words have given you biblical lifelines and helped you access more of God's abundance in your SHE journey. We've offered you a SHE bracelet with nine new charms representing your life as a safe, healthy, and empowered woman:

* Protection

* Intimacy

* Femininity

* Beauty

* Purity

* Freedom

* Mentorship

* Boundaries

* Purpose

As you glance back at those charms, some will mean more to you than others. Some may even fall by the wayside. It'll be up to you to make sure each one is secure, and you'll need to continue to add new charms through each phase of life. It will even be up to you whether or not you wear your SHE bracelet proudly as evidence that God's work in you is the lasting kind.

The choice is yours. But we hope you will join us on this remarkable adventure to SHEdom.

Choosing the SHE Path

We've gotten to know several SHE women found in the Bible. We saw how . . .

❉ Hagar found protection through God;

❉ Mary of Bethany and Mary of Magdala found intimacy with Christ;

❉ Deborah found her femininity by being gentle and quiet—but spirited;

❉ Bathsheba found unfading beauty through forgiveness;

❉ Mary, the mother of Jesus, walked in purity;

❉ Rahab became free by breaking the curse and living the blessing;

❉ Ruth found guidance, support, and accountability through her mentor;

❉ Wisdom walked with God and now invites us to walk boundaried with her;

❉ Esther lived a life of purpose for such a time as this.

Now before we leave you, we'd like to talk about two more women mentioned in the Bible. They aren't like the other nine, who lived in distant lands. These two live in the animal kingdom. They're the she-ostrich and the she-eagle. Here's what Job has to say about the ostrich:

> *The ostrich flaps her wings futilely—all those beautiful feathers, but useless! She lays her eggs on the hard ground, leaves them there in the dirt, exposed to the weather, not caring that they might get stepped on and cracked or trampled by some wild animal. She's negligent with her young, as if they weren't even hers. She cares nothing about anything. She wasn't created very smart, that's for sure, wasn't given her share of good sense. But when she runs, oh, how she runs, laughing, leaving horse and rider in the dust.*
>
> **Job 39:13-18,** MSG

We became intrigued with these verses, and a trip to the library helped us discover why God chose to talk about the ostrich as He did. This is what we found.

The largest of all birds, ostriches live mostly in the sandy parts of Africa. Their long strides make them the fastest of all birds, moving up to forty miles per hour. They eat almost anything they can find, and they learn to outrun their natural enemies.

The mother ostrich is a polygamous bird. Several females mate with one male and lay their clutches of eggs in a communal nest consisting of between fifteen and sixty eggs in shallow depressions on the ground. Many times the female ostrich will abandon her eggs once her job of laying them is through, and the male then takes over to keep them warm. Because the nest is built in such a vulnerable place, the eggs are often stepped on or eaten by other animals. The babies that do make it to hatching often find themselves in a busy, frittering, noisy world.

Contrast that to the eagle.

Did you command the eagle's flight, and teach her to build her nest in the heights, perfectly at home on the high cliff-face, invulnerable on pinnacle and crag? From her perch she searches for prey, spies it at a great distance.

Job 39:27-29, MSG

The eagle builds her nest way up in inaccessible places. She mates for life and often returns to the same nest year after year, adding to it each time she returns. One eagle's nest found in Ohio was used for thirty-six years and weighed almost one ton. The she-eagle incubates the eggs for a long period of time, and once the babies hatch, she protects and teaches them for as long as 130 days before she sends them out on their own. The whole reproductive cycle may last for up to twelve months.

Perhaps the most amazing characteristic of the she-eagle is her vision. Her keen eyesight allows her to see up to the length of two football fields. The ostrich also has keen eyes, which are protected by long lashes. But unlike the eagle, reality is restricted only to what she can see, touch, hear, smell, or feel around her. While the eagle remains aware of what's out *there*, the ostrich stays busy only with what's *here*. From the eagle's point of view, she can see where to go for what's good and where to avoid the bad. Where to find food and where to shun danger. The eagle has a clear understanding not only of what's below, but also what's above. She lives every day of her life from the high places with her eagle-eye view.

As we see it, you and I can choose whether will be more like the ostrich or the eagle in two distinct areas: perspective and commitment. Let us explain.

Perspective

The difference between the ostrich's and the eagle's perspective can be summed up by what K. P. Yohannan, president of Gospel for Asia, calls horizontal thinking versus vertical thinking. He describes horizontal thinking as focusing on the small scope of vision directly surrounding a person. It includes immediate needs, such as physical weariness, hunger, and discomfort. On the flip side, vertical thinking keeps the attention on God's big-picture perspective of eternity. Vertical thinking concerns itself with reaching out to others and growing in God's love, understanding that life here is only a small part of eternity.[2]

You and I have issues and problems and challenges and questions. All of these are important, and God wants us to go to Him for direction in all of them. We've done that in nine areas throughout this book. But when we stare at the problems around us and make them our focal points, we overlook the bigger picture God wants us to be a part of—helping others get to know Jesus. As godly women, when we become ostrich-eyed, horizontal shes, we do what Yohannan calls "forgetting the war going on behind the scenes and interpreting everything in our lives through the filter of our five senses."[3]

But we are not created for time. We are created for eternity. We are created for vertical focus—to love and know Jesus well, and then to introduce others to Him. The thing is, when we're vertically sighted and when we're occupied with serving God and others, we're in a better place to hear what He has to say about all the other things—protection, intimacy, femininity, beauty, purity, freedom, mentorship, boundaries, and purpose.

Vertical-mindedness encourages us to look less at the dos and don'ts and more at God Himself. When we turn our eagle eyes on God, we know how we need to live our life.

LYNDA ✳ When I was a child, my dad worked for the post office in our town. He kept his work car parked outside the garage whenever he wasn't driving his rural delivery route. In order to ward off ice and snow during those cold Ohio winters, Dad put a piece of cardboard on his windshield. In the morning, he started the motor, removed the cardboard, then went about his day. If he'd kept the cardboard there, he never could have seen to go forward. ✳

Horizontal focus does the same thing. It puts the everyday issues of life right in the center of our view so we can't see anything more of what God wants us to accomplish or anywhere else He wants us to go. But vertical sight daily keeps us giving God the cardboard of our needs so it doesn't impair our view, and fixing our sights on ways He wants us to grow and things He wants us to do—while He's working on our needs. Get it? We spend our energy serving Him and loving others while He takes care of us.

REBECCA ✳ My seventeen-year-old brother, Luke, and I recently had a revealing conversation in the kitchen of our family's farmhouse. We expressed how we both wanted to grow closer to God and connect with Him deeply. We discussed how easy it is to fall into the trap of learning *about* God without really getting to *know* Him personally. I shared that doing this is like getting on the Internet and finding all you can about your favorite movie or sports star but never having a relationship with that person. ✳

Let's not miss the point: The point is God Himself. Each one of these nine aspects of a true SHE woman is an avenue through which you and I can be drawn deeper into relationship with God. If all this book has done is give you more head knowledge, then it has failed. On the other hand, if it has nudged you to give aspects of your life to Him more completely or caused you to better understand His loving plan for you, then it has succeeded.

Commitment

The ostrich's horizontal thinking causes her to abandon her nest when better things come along. The eagle's vertical thinking requires that she stay with the job until it's done.

We live in a fickle world. Go from this diet to that. Switch from this church to that one. Concentrate on one thing and then another. But that's not what making a commitment to God is about.

Commit is what the Hebrews 11 heroes of the faith did:

> *These people all died having faith in God. They did not receive what God had promised to them. But they could see far ahead to all the things God promised and they were glad for them. They knew they were strangers here. This earth was not their home. People who say these things show they are looking for a country of their own. They did not think about the country they had come from. If they had, they might have gone back. But they wanted a better country. And so God is not ashamed to be called their God. He has made a city for them.*
>
> **Hebrews 11:13-16,** NLV

Commit is what you can do too. The very idea of a relationship with God may be new to you. Or you might have dabbled in mediocrity so far in your Christian life. A little of this faith, a little of that hope. Walking the walk only in an accepting crowd. Refusing to go deeper with God. But it's time to commit—irrevocably, unequivocally, most assuredly.

When we commit to commitment, we do what may be called "crossing the Rubicon." This historical reference dates back to 49 BC and the Rubicon River in northern Italy that formed part of the boundary between Cisalpine Gaul and Italy. When Julius Caesar crossed the Rubicon, his act was regarded by the senate as an irreversible proclamation of war. Since then, crossing the Rubicon has come to mean the "limiting line; one that when crossed commits a person irrevocably."[4]

In his book *The Life God Blesses*, author Gordon MacDonald talks about different ways we can respond after a spiritual experience and how that response determines whether or not the change for the better will stick. He defines *spirituality* as "walking with Christ, being filled with the Spirit, and living abundantly."[5] The *spiritual experience*, on the other hand, is merely to enjoy a spiritual high and then to come down again and resume life as usual. MacDonald writes, "Spirituality is like a well that produces and produces and produces with long-term profitability. But a spiritual experience is like a well . . . with initial impressive performance but only short-term viability."[6]

So where do you go from here? Will your SHE identity endure and create lasting changes in your life, or will you settle for a sugar high and soon come plunging down?

Commitment is the difference between true spirituality and mere spiritual experience. The difference between lasting, abundant life and only a temporary change is your willingness to commit. You must be willing to forget what lies behind and keep your vertical eyes on the One who has been and will be committed to providing what's best for you every second of your life.

Today we want to help you cross your Rubicon. Through this prayer, you can make a forever, covenant commitment with God to walk forward and upward with Him—from now until you stand before Him face-to-face:

Dear Lord,

I choose today (date) _____

to put my hand in Yours forever and to allow You to lead me across the Rubicon. Let this day signal a new and better and richer and lasting spiritual beginning for me. I won't settle for a lukewarm Christian life. From now on, I will not only look forward to the delight of eternity with You, but I will enjoy the fulfillment and peace of an intimate journey with You here on earth. I want the changes You make in me to be lasting ones that glorify You and encourage others to also turn to You. I long to grow as the safe, healthy, and empowered SHE You want me to be. I desire to be protected, capable of true intimacy, and be able to effectively balance tough and tender femininity. I crave the understanding of what it means to be truly beautiful, living in purity and freedom. I will seek to be mentored, boundaried, and purposeful in the way I live my life from this point forward. I'm excited about the continued adventure that You and I will walk together. These are Your gifts to me, and my gift to You is my forever, unretractable commitment to follow You wherever You lead. Thanks for my new SHE life in You. In the name of Jesus Christ, amen.

✳

"I made you thrive like a plant in the field; and you grew, matured, and became very beautiful. . . . I spread My wing over you and covered your nakedness. Yes, I swore an oath to you and entered into a covenant with you, and you became Mine," says the Lord God. . . . I adorned you with ornaments, put bracelets on your wrists, and a chain on your neck. . . . Thus you were adorned with gold and silver, and your clothing was of fine linen, silk, and embroidered cloth. You ate pastry of fine flour, honey, and oil. You were exceedingly beautiful, and succeeded to royalty. Your fame went out among the nations because of your beauty, for it was perfect through My splendor which I had bestowed on you," says the Lord God.

Ezekiel 16:7-8, 11, 13-14, NKJV

Our friends and fellow SHEs, our sisters beautiful through God's splendor, may you continue to live life vertically, knowing God's truth, which always refutes Satan's lies to you. Keep your eyes focused on things above, and don't get distracted by things below. Stay committed to the journey—run with endurance, and lay aside the things that slow you down.

And if we don't get to meet you this side of heaven, we'll see you at journey's end, where all of history's SHEs will gather and together worship Jesus—the One who makes a she . . . SHE.

✳ **SHEism** ✳ SHE is every woman who seeks more from God and submits her life to His transforming work and a lifetime of being reborn into God's original design.

ENDNOTES

Introduction
1. Psalm 71:20; Romans 12:2; Philippians 3:21; Colossians 1:6; 1 Peter 5:10-11
2. John 10:10

Chapter 1
1. Carole Mayhall, *From the Heart of a Woman* (Colorado Springs: NavPress, 1976), 10–11.
2. Cathi Hanauer, *The Bitch in the House* (New York: HarperCollins, 2002), front flap. Please excuse the crude title.
3. Ibid.
4. Danielle Crittenden, *What Our Mothers Didn't Tell Us: Why Happiness Eludes the Modern Woman* (New York: Touchstone, 2000), back cover.
5. Ibid.
6. John 15:9-11; Psalm 25:3; John 14:27
7. John 8:44
8. John 16:24
9. John 8:44
10. John 8:32
11. Genesis 2:18, NKJV
12. Psalm 91:4
13. Jeremiah 30:17
14. 3 John 1:2, NASB
15. Psalm 68:35

Chapter 2
1. Joni Eareckson Tada, *A Quiet Place in a Crazy World* (Sisters, Ore.: Multnomah Books, 1993), 36–37.

2. John Eldredge, *Wild at Heart* (Nashville: Thomas Nelson, 2001), 16–17.
3. Genesis 16:7-8
4. Genesis 16:13
5. Romans 8:28
6. 1 Peter 5:8, NIV
7. 1 Peter 3:8
8. Proverbs 11:14, NKJV
9. Luke 22:31-32
10. Hebrews 6:19
11. Matthew 24:35
12. Revelation 3:20
13. Exodus 2:2-3

Chapter 3
1. Cynthia Heald, *Intimacy with God* (Colorado Springs: NavPress, 2000), 23.
2. All statistics taken from the Barna Group Web site, www.barna.org.
3. Psalm 27:8; 139:1; John 3:16-17; 7:37-38; Romans 5:8
4. A. W. Tozer, *Best of Tozer* (Grand Rapids, Mich.: Baker Books, 1978), 162.
5. Calvin Miller, *Into the Depths of God* (Minneapolis: Bethany House, 2000), 23.
6. Genesis 2:18
7. Genesis 3:16
8. Larry Crabb, *Soul Talk* (Nashville: Integrity Publishing, 2003), 13.
9. U.S. divorce statistics reported on DivorceMagazine.com Web site. Sources: U.S. Census Bureau, National Center for Health Statistics, Americans for Divorce

Reform, Centers for Disease Control and Prevention, Institute for Equality in Marriage, American Association for Single People, Ameristat, and Public Agenda.

10 *Psychology Today*, seventh ed. (New York: McGraw-Hill, 1991), 425–428.

11 Ibid.

12 Exodus 15:26; Psalm 147:3; Jeremiah 31:3-4

13 Luke 10:38-42

14 Luke 10:41-42

15 John 11:1-44

16 John 11:32

17 Matthew 26:6-13; Mark 14:3-9; John 12:1-11

18 John 12:8

19 Luke 8:2

20 Mark 15:40-41; John 19:25

21 Mark 16:1; Luke 24:1, 10

22 John 20:16

23 John 20:17

24 Michael Phillips, *A God to Call Father* (Wheaton, Ill.: Tyndale House Publishers, Inc., 1994).

25 David Blakenhorn, *Fatherless America* (New York: HarperCollins, 1996), 1.

26 Gary Smalley, *Secrets to Lasting Love* (New York: Simon and Schuster, 2000), 28–31.

Chapter 4

1 Emily Barnes, publication unknown

2 Gary Smalley and John Trent, *The Two Sides of Love* (Colorado Springs: Focus on the Family Publishing, 1990).

3 Betty Friedan, *The Feminine Mystique*, twentieth anniversary ed. (New York: W. W. Norton and Company, 1983), 364.

4 Diane Passno, *Feminism: Mystique or Mistake?* (Wheaton, Ill.: Tyndale House Publishers, 2000), 29.

5 Ibid., 31–32.

6 *Merriam-Webster's Collegiate Dictionary*, eleventh ed. (Springfield, Mass: Merriam-Webster, Inc., 2003).

7 Danielle Crittenden, *What Our Mothers Didn't Tell Us* (New York: Simon and Schuster, 1999), 14.

8 Ibid., 22.

9 William J. Bennett, *The Book of Virtues* (New York: Simon and Schuster, 1993), 633.

10 Elizabeth Fox-Genovese, *Feminism Is Not the Story of My Life* (New York: Doubleday, 1996).

11 Isaiah 40:10-11, NIV

12 Matthew 25:21

13 2 Chronicles 20:15

14 Judges 4:14

15 Hebrews 11:32

16 1 Peter 5:5, NKJV

17 Ephesians 5:25-29

18 1 Peter 4:10

19 Judges 4:14

20 1 John 4:4

21 Judges 5:2, 31

22 Judges 5:31

Chapter 5

1 Leslie Ludy, *Authentic Beauty* (Sisters, Ore.: Multnomah Publishers, 2003), 5.

2 Lois W. Banner, *American Beauty* (New York: Knopf Publishing, 1983), 13.

3 Naomi Wolf, *The Beauty Myth: How Images of Beauty Are Used Against Women* (New York: Doubleday, 1991), 10.

4 John Eldredge, *Wild at Heart* (Nashville: Thomas Nelson, 2001), 16–17.

5 1 Samuel 16:7

6 1 Peter 3:3-4

7 1 Samuel 13:14

8 1 Kings 15:5

9 2 Samuel 12:10, 15-18; 13:28-29; 18:14-15; 1 Kings 2:24-25

[10] Proverbs 31:10

[11] Proverbs 31:30

[12] 1 Corinthians 6:19-20

[13] Philippians 4:8

[14] Matthew 6:19-21

[15] 2 Corinthians 4:16

[16] *UCB Devotional* (Australia: United Christian Broadcasters), 39. Author and copyright date unknown.

Chapter 6

[1] Elisabeth Elliot, *Passion and Purity* (Grand Rapids, Mich.: Fleming H. Revell and Co., 1984), 21.

[2] James 1:15

[3] Genesis 3:6, NIV

[4] Genesis 2:16-17

[5] Judges 14:1, NASB

[6] Judges 14:3, NASB

[7] Judges 16:4-31

[8] 1 Corinthians 6:18

[9] Tony Campolo, "Sex Ed's Failure Rate," *Christianity Today* (February 3, 1993), 22.

[10] Rebecca St. James, *Wait for Me* (Nashville: Thomas Nelson, 2002).

[11] *Merriam-Webster's Collegiate Dictionary*, eleventh ed. (Springfield, Mass.: Merriam-Webster, Inc., 2003).

[12] Ed Young, *Pure Sex* (Sisters, Ore.: Multnomah Publishers, 1997), 9.

[13] *Seventeen*, August 2003. Title and page unknown.

[14] Ibid.

[15] Richard Foster, *Money, Sex, and Power* (Dallas: Word Publishing, 1985).

[16] Randy Alcorn, *The Purity Principle* (Sisters, Ore.: Multnomah Publishers, 2003), 15–16.

[17] Ibid., 10.

[18] Charles R. Swindoll, *Sanctity of Life* (Nashville: Word Publishing, 1990), 57–58.

[19] Luke 1:26-38; Romans 1:1-4

[20] Luke 2:1-7

[21] Luke 2:19

[22] Leviticus 12; Luke 2:21-38

[23] Luke 2:41-52, NIV

[24] Acts 1:14

[25] Luke 1:38, KJV

[26] Luke 1:43

[27] 2 Timothy 2:21

[28] Luke 1:28, NKJV

[29] Psalm 24:3-4

[30] Proverbs 6:27-28

[31] Romans 8:37

[32] Deuteronomy 11:19

[33] 1 John 1:9

Chapter 7

[1] Barbara Johnson, contributor, *The Women of Faith Devotional* (Grand Rapids, Mich.: Zondervan, 2002), 211.

[2] Matthew 18:35, AMP

[3] John 10:10; 14:27; 15:11; 17:13

[4] Genesis 3:16

[5] Genesis 3:17-19

[6] Exodus 34:7

[7] Ezekiel 18:1-4

[8] Psalm 119:43, 45. See also Psalm 116:16; 124:7-8; Colossians 2:20; and Revelation 12:11.

[9] Proverbs 26:2

[10] Genesis 9:18-25

[11] Gien Karssen, *Her Name Is Woman: Book 1* (Colorado Springs: NavPress, 1975), 71.

[12] Joshua 2:12-18

[13] Isaiah 1:18, NIV

[14] Hebrews 11:31

[15] Numbers 22–24

[16] 2 Corinthians 10:4

[17] As heard by author in a church sermon. Additional source information is unknown.

Chapter 8

[1] Betty Huizenga, *Gifts of Gold: Gathering, Training, and Encouraging Mentors* (Colorado Springs: David C. Cook Publishing, 2002), 25.

[2] 2 Timothy 2:2

[3] Howard G. Hendricks, *As Iron Sharpens Iron: Building Character in a Mentoring Relationship* (Chicago: Moody Press, 1995), 18.

[4] Ted Engstrom, *The Fine Art of Mentoring: Passing on to Others What God Has Given to You* (Brentwood, Tenn.: Wolgemuth and Hyatt, 1989), 4.

[5] Huizenga, 27.

[6] Matthew 2:1-11

[7] Gien Karssen, *Her Name Is Woman: Book 2* (Colorado Springs: NavPress, 1977), 133.

[8] Luke 2:14, NASB

[9] Hendricks, 63.

[10] Ruth 1:9-14, NIV

[11] Proverbs 27:17

Chapter 9

[1] Barbara Johnson, *The Women of Faith Devotional* (Grand Rapids, Mich.: Zondervan, 2002), 211.

[2] Rick Hampson, *USA Today* (March 26, 2002): 01A.

[3] Hans Selye, *Stress without Distress* (New York: J. B. Lippincott Co., 1974).

[4] Henry Cloud and John Townsend, *Boundaries* (Grand Rapids, Mich.: Zondervan, 1992), 29.

[5] Randy Alcorn, *The Purity Principle* (Sisters, Ore.: Multnomah Publishers, 2003), 28.

[6] Henry Cloud and John Townsend, *Safe People* (Grand Rapids, Mich.: Zondervan, 1995).

[7] Proverbs 8:22-26

[8] Proverbs 8:27-29

[9] Proverbs 8:30

[10] Proverbs 8:32-34

[11] John 1:1-3

[12] Proverbs 8:35

[13] St. James, *Wait for Me*, 123-124.

Chapter 10

[1] Bill Peel and Kathy Peel, *Discover Your Destiny* (Colorado Springs: NavPress, 1996).

[2] Gillian Tett, *Financial Times* (May 13-14, 2000): 3.

[3] Psalm 33:11

[4] Genesis 1:6-24

[5] Colossians 1:16, MSG

[6] Rick Warren, *The Purpose-Driven Life* (Grand Rapids, Mich.: Zondervan, 2002).

[7] Psalm 139, NIV

[8] Jeremiah 29:11-13

[9] Genesis 1:27

[10] Romans 8:29

[11] Genesis 1:28

[12] Psalm 100:2

[13] Hebrews 11:9, AMP

[14] Gordon MacDonald, *Renewing Your Spiritual Passion* (Nashville: Thomas Nelson, 1985), 71-82, italics added.

[15] Ibid., 37-64.

[16] *Psychology* (New York: McGraw-Hill, 1992), 564.

[17] Esther 4:14, NKJV

[18] Esther 4:16, NIV

[19] Esther 8:17

[20] Romans 8:28

Chapter 11

[1] Hannah Hurnard, *Hinds' Feet on High Places* (Wheaton, Ill.: Tyndale House Publishers, Inc., 1975), 235.

[2] K. P. Yohannan, *Living in Light of Eternity: Your Life Can Make a Difference* (Grand Rapids, Mich.: Chosen Publishers, 1995), 19.

[3] Ibid., 22.

[4] *Merriam-Webster's Collegiate Dictionary*, eleventh ed. (Springfield, Mass.: Merriam-Webster, Inc., 2003).

[5] Gordon MacDonald, *The Life God Blesses: Weathering the Storms of Life That Threaten the Soul* (Nashville: Thomas Nelson, 1997), 48.

[6] Ibid., 52.